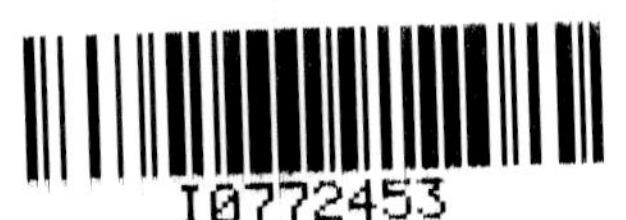

mermaid coloring book

F. FRANKLIN

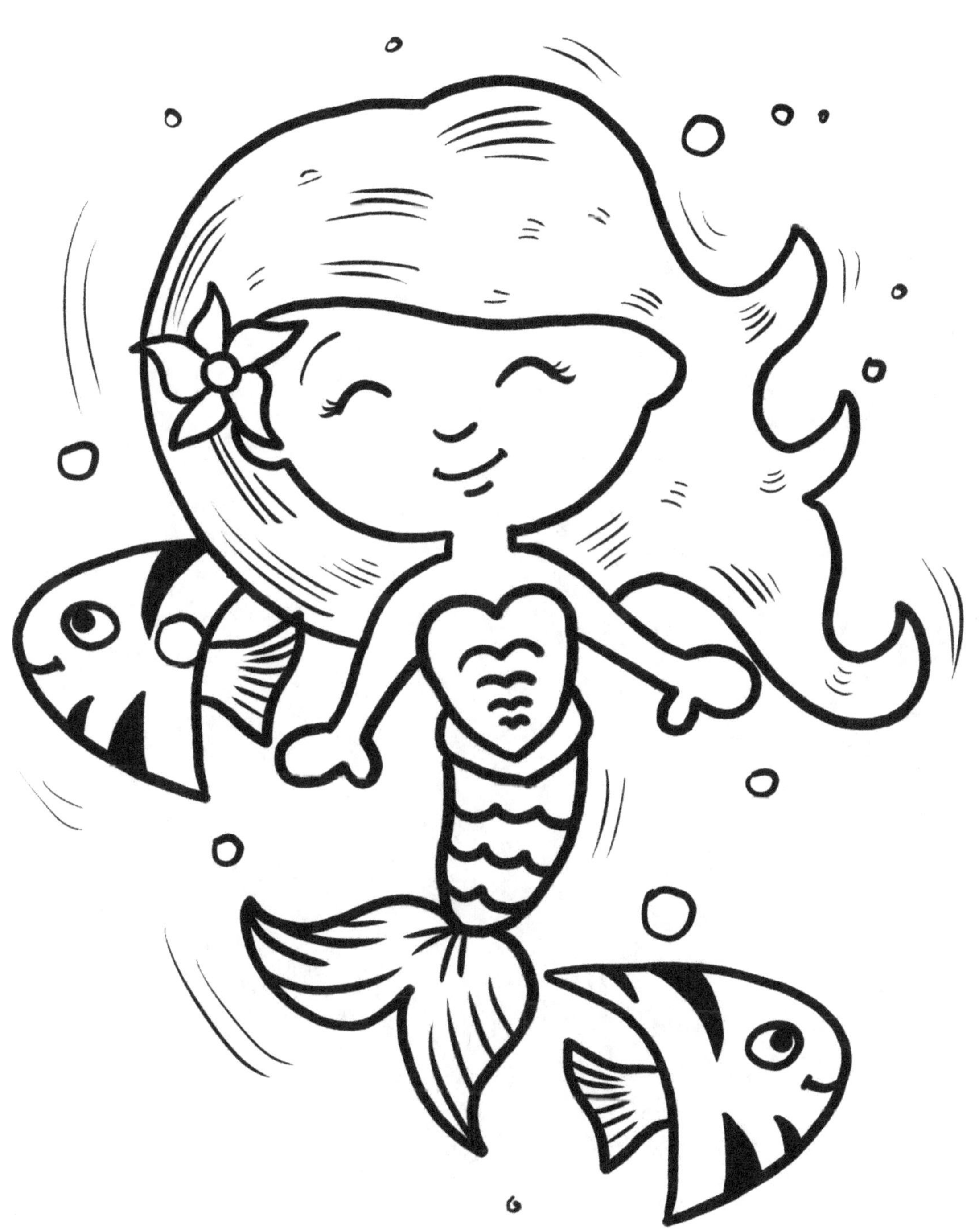

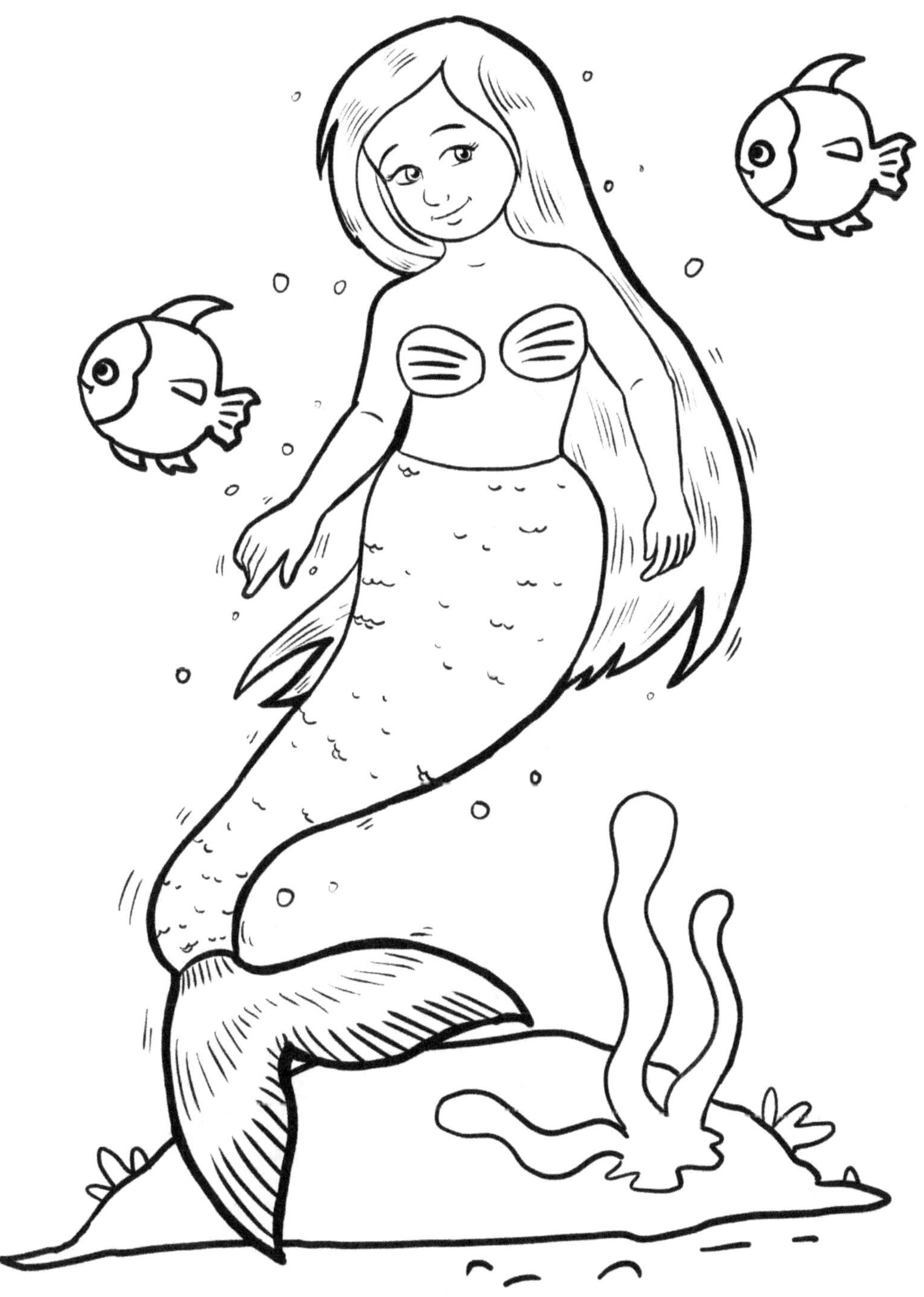

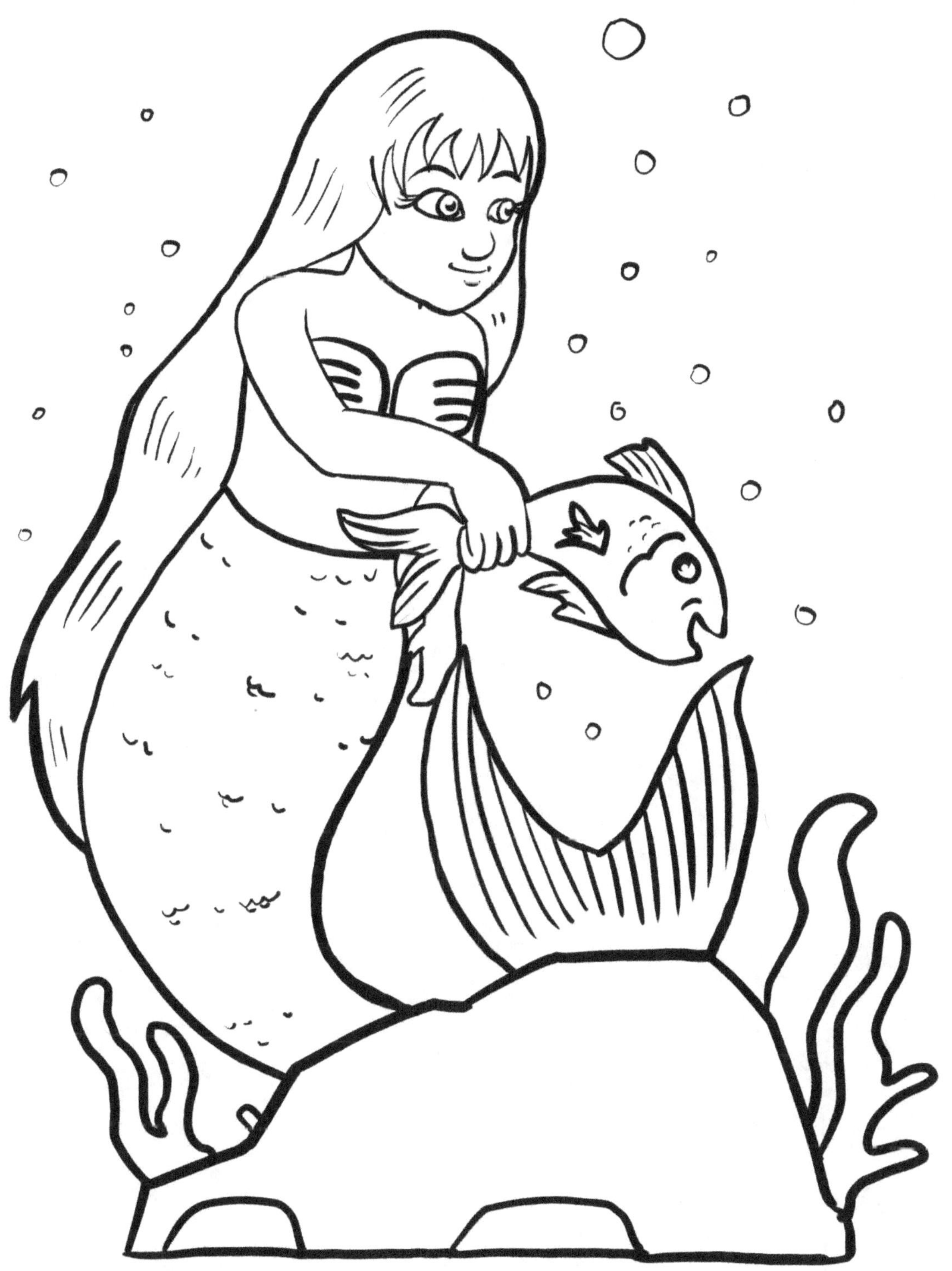

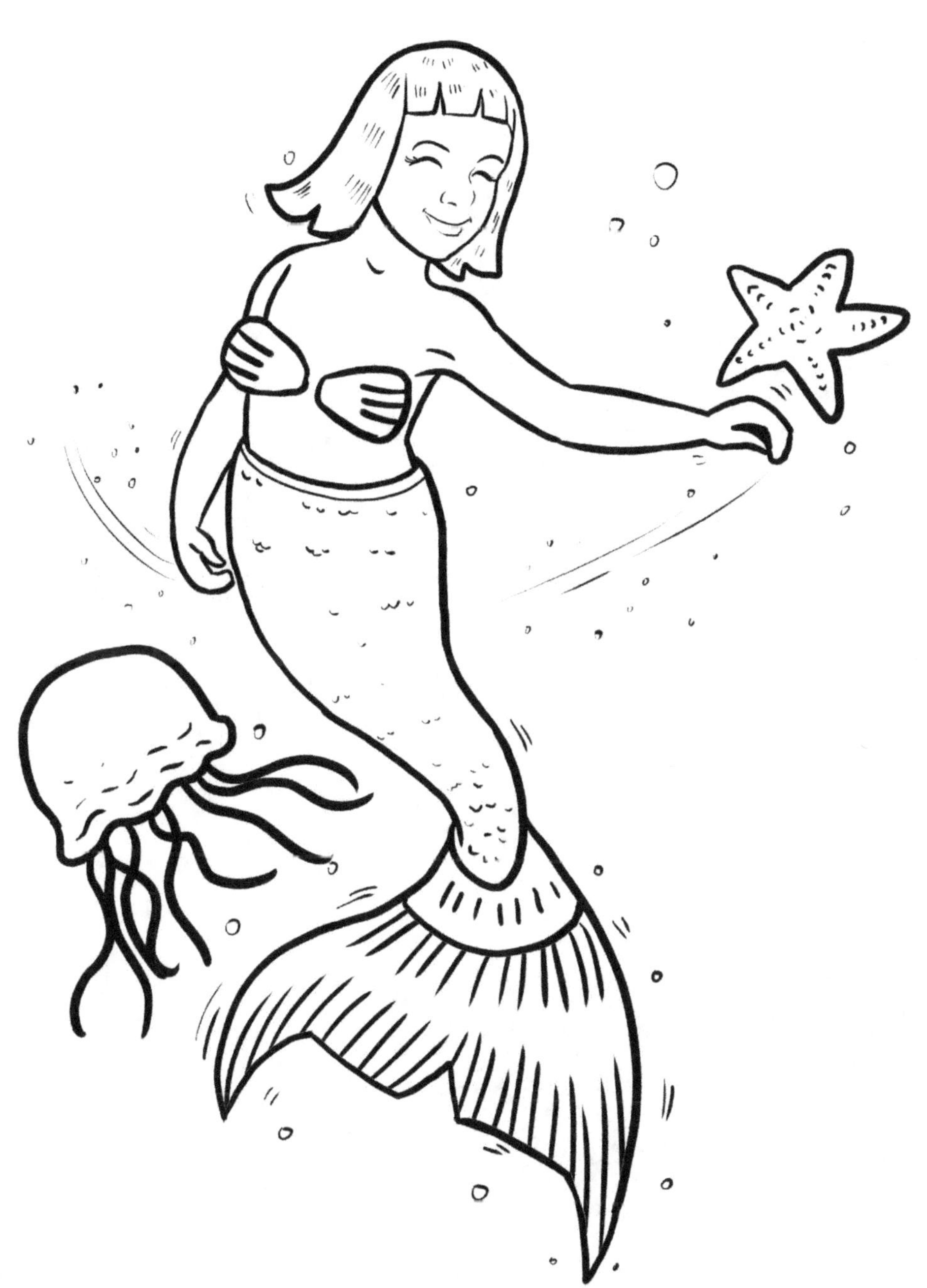

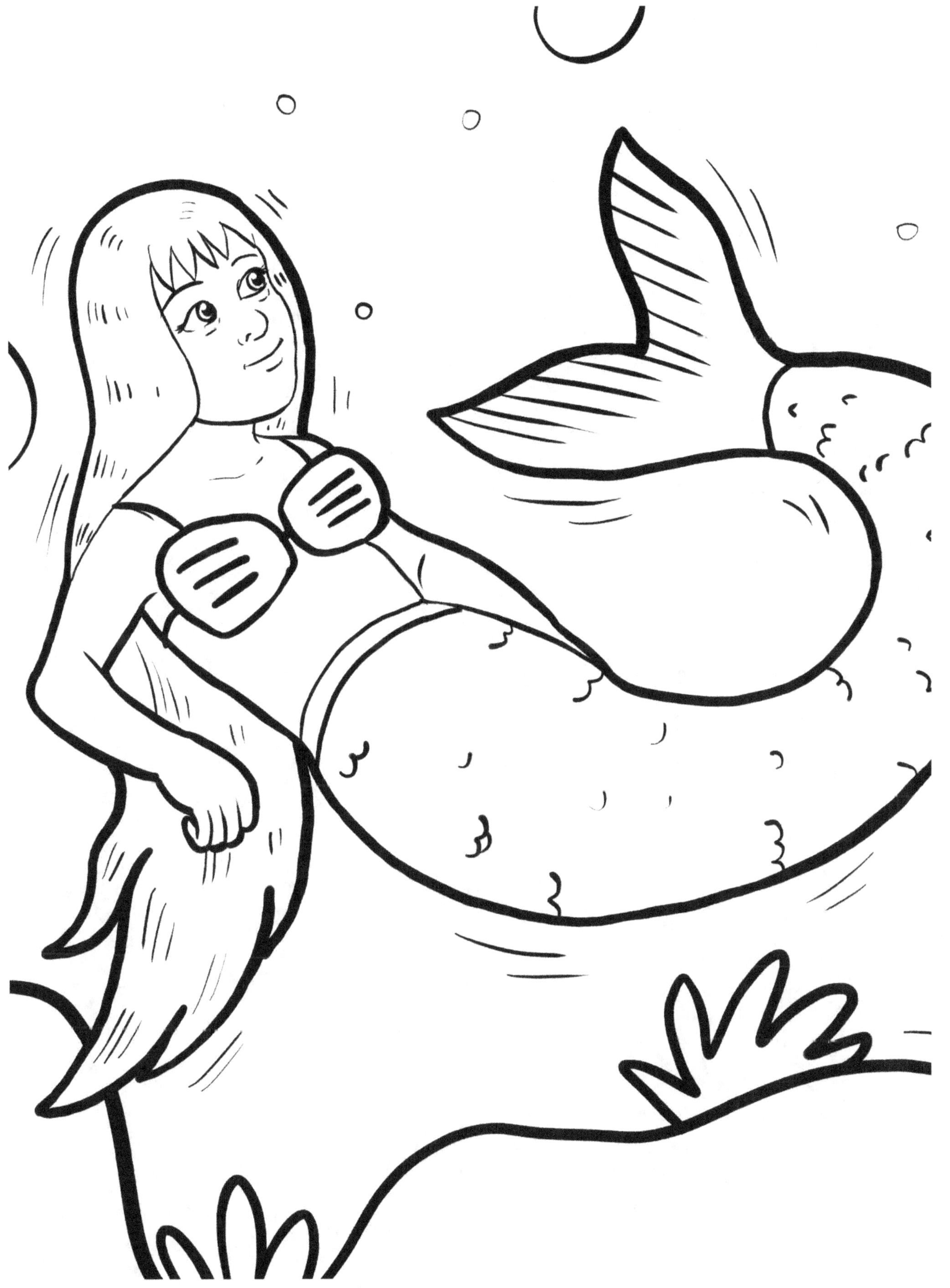

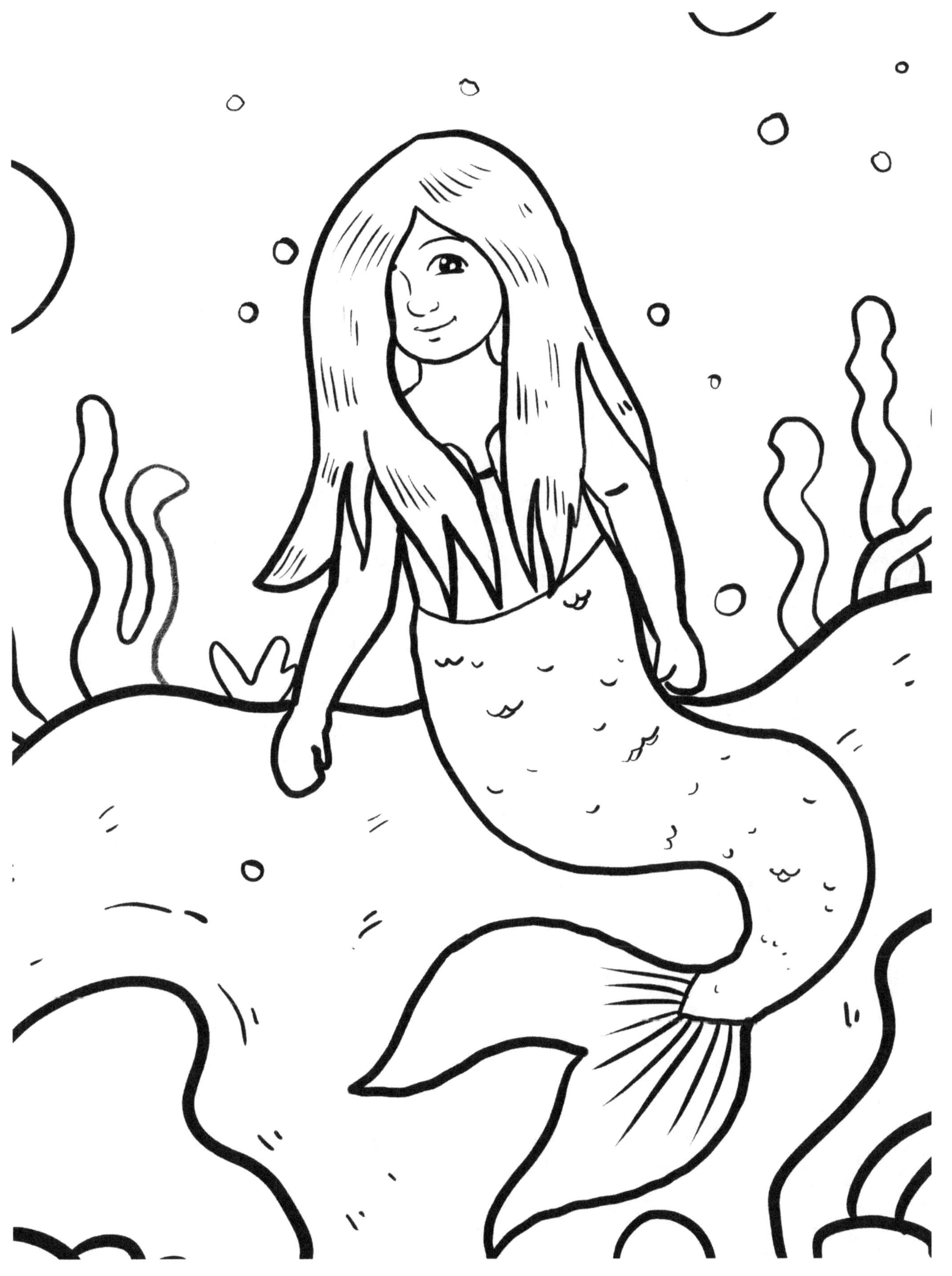

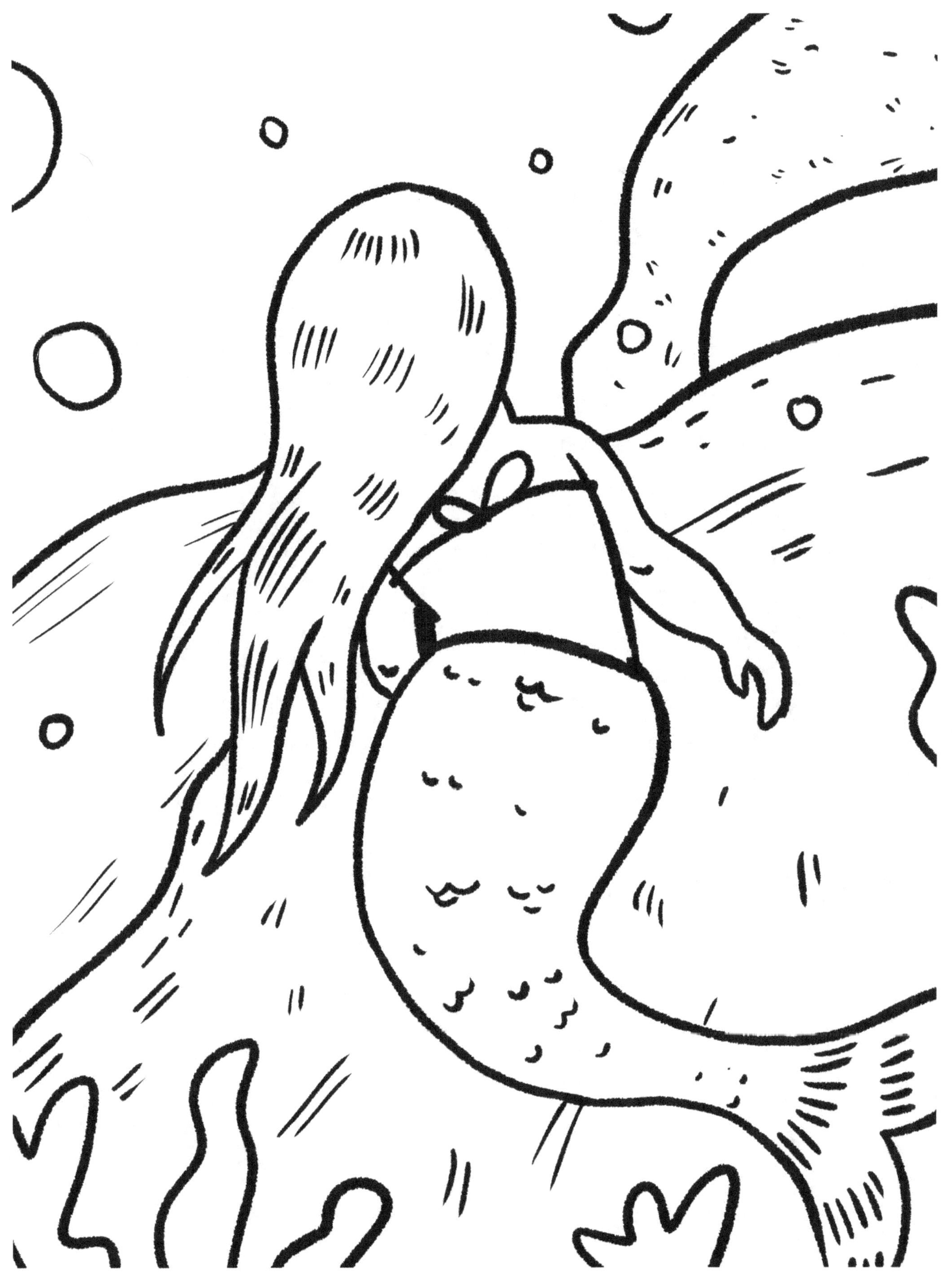

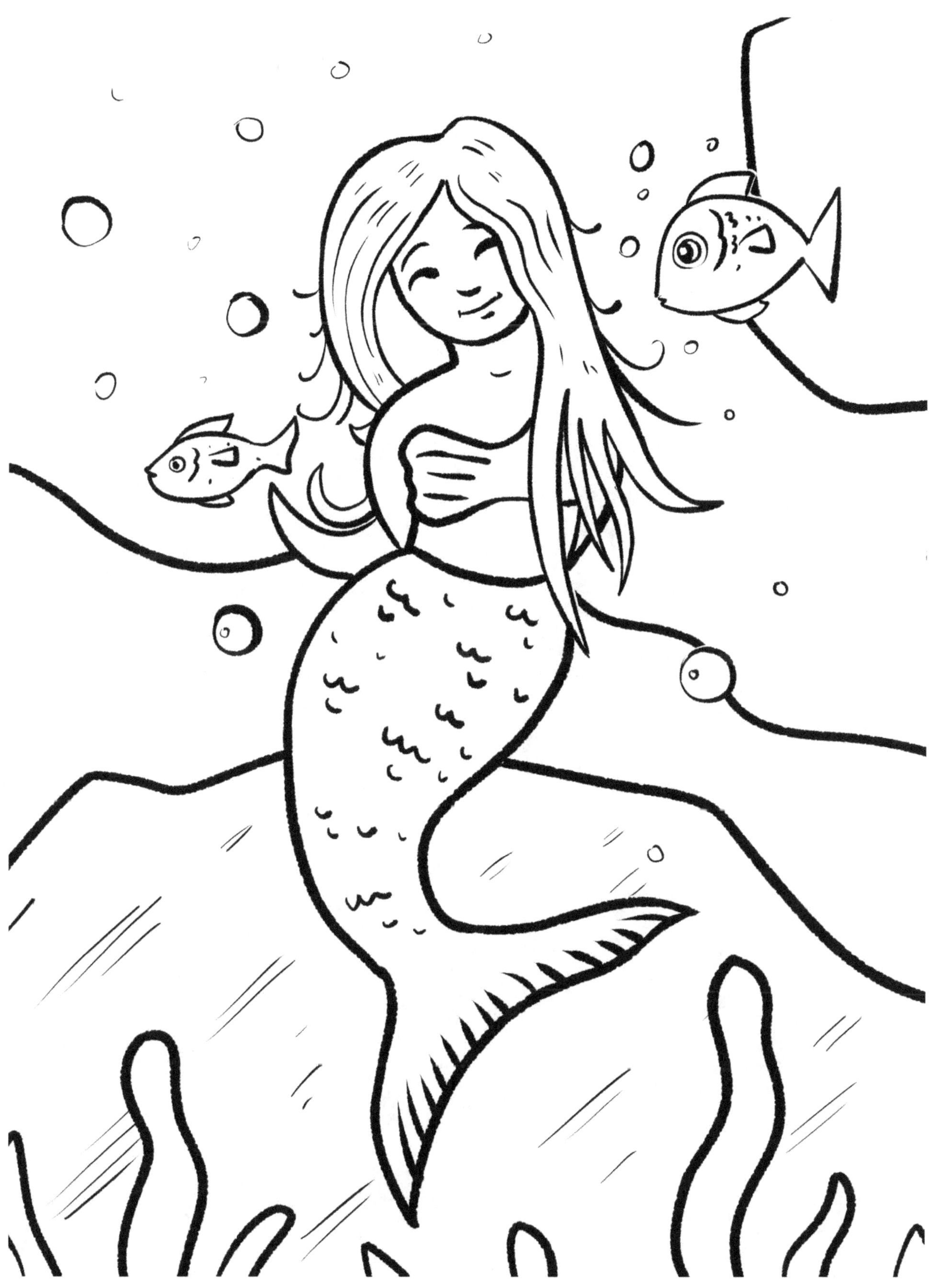

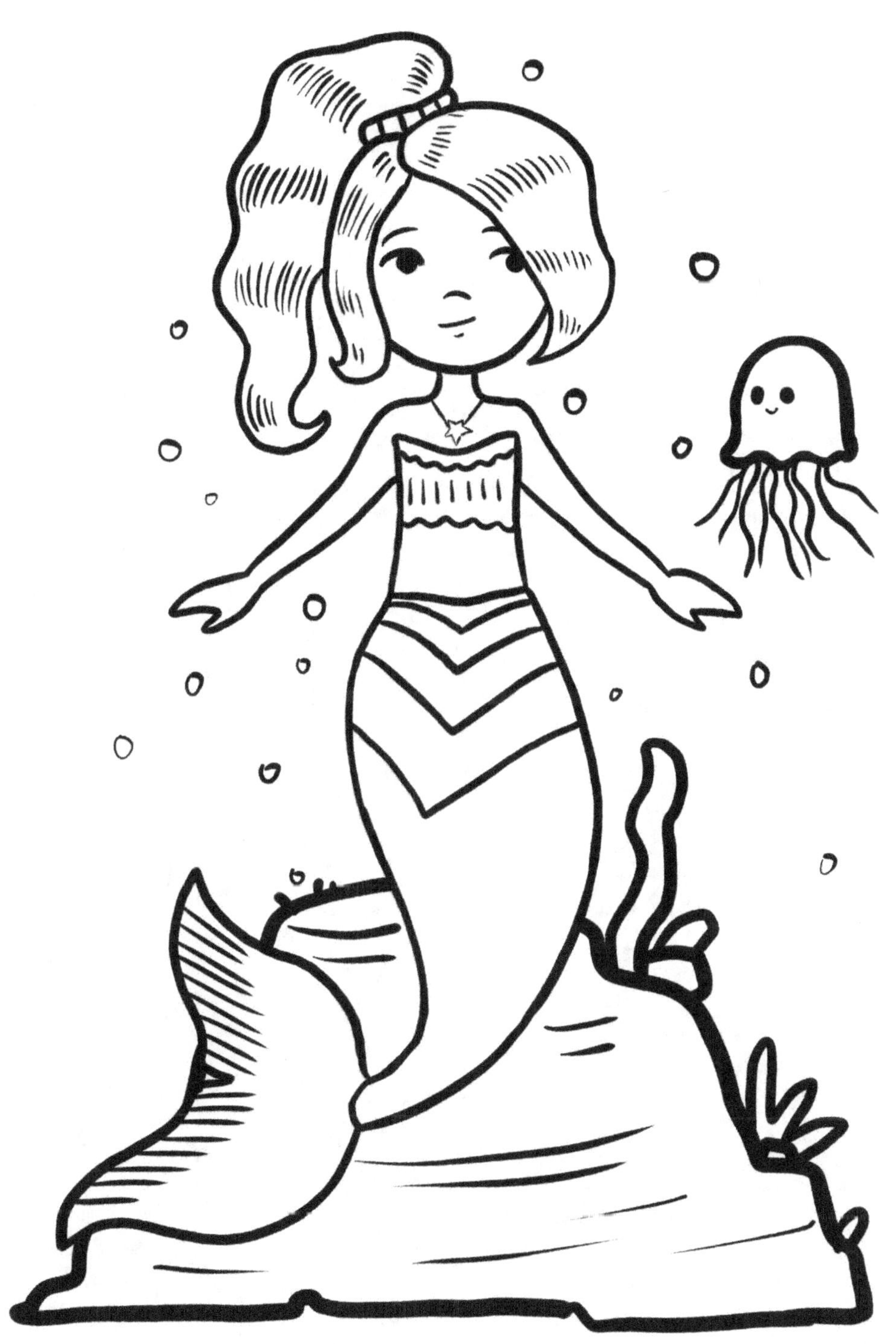

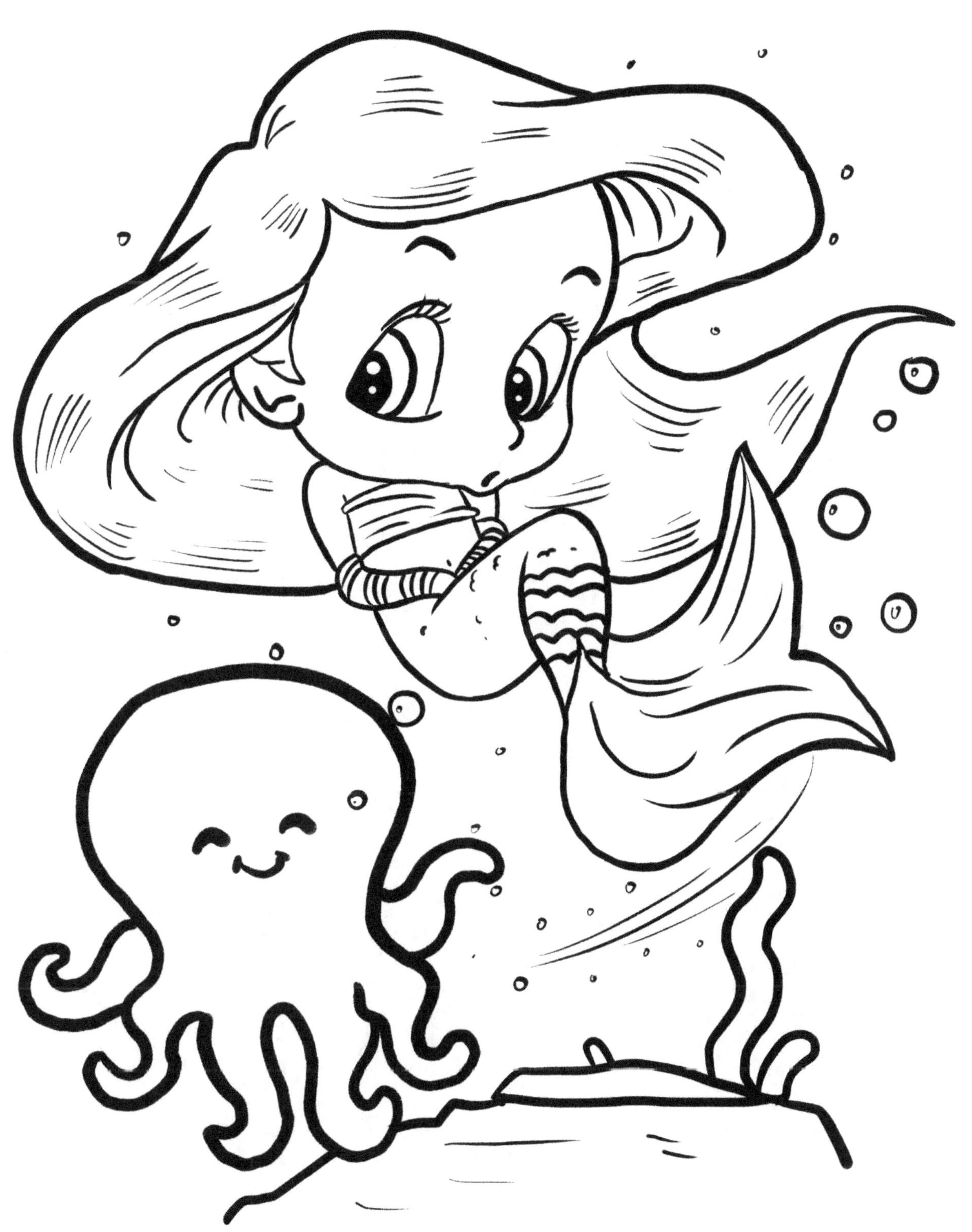

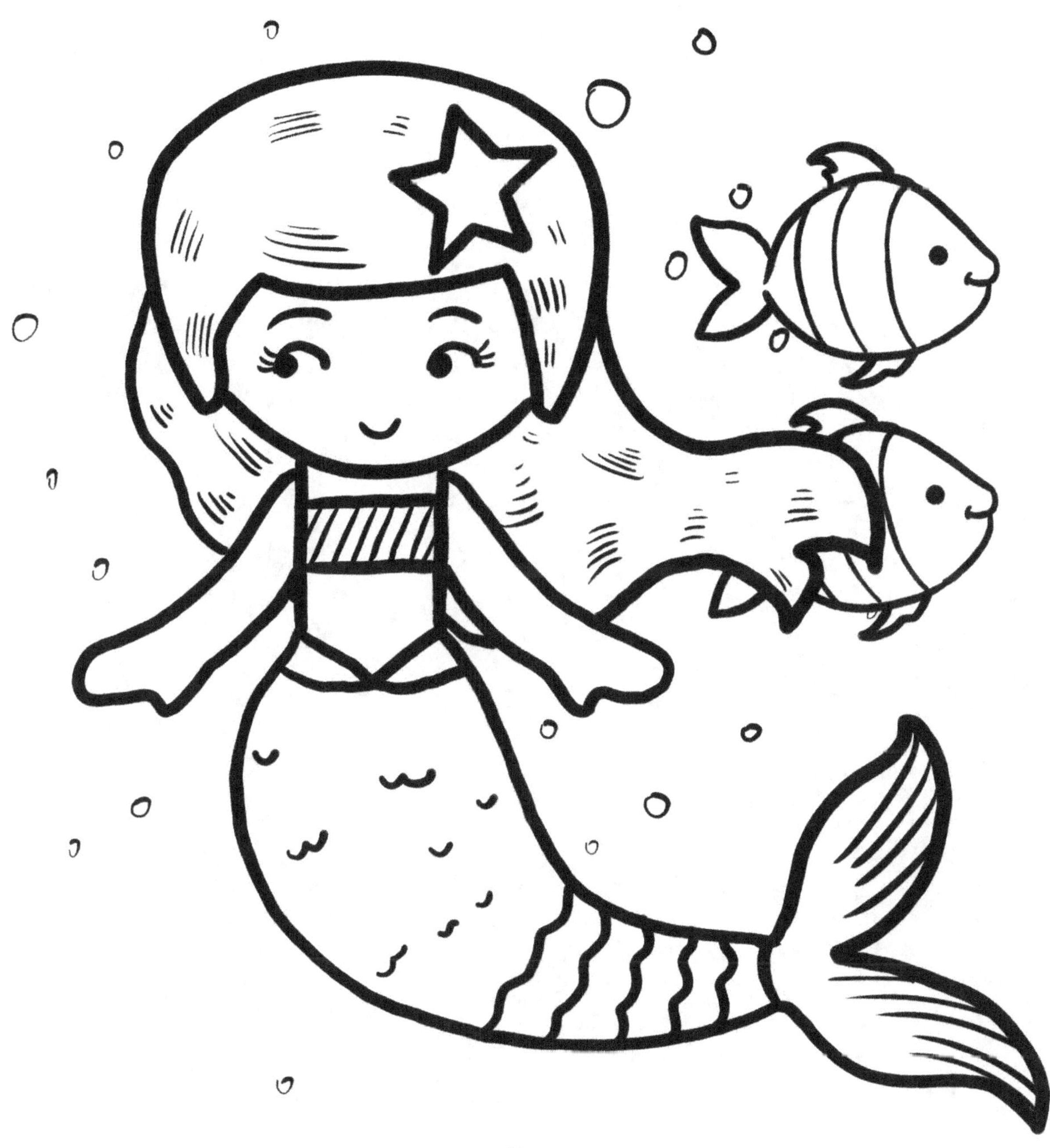

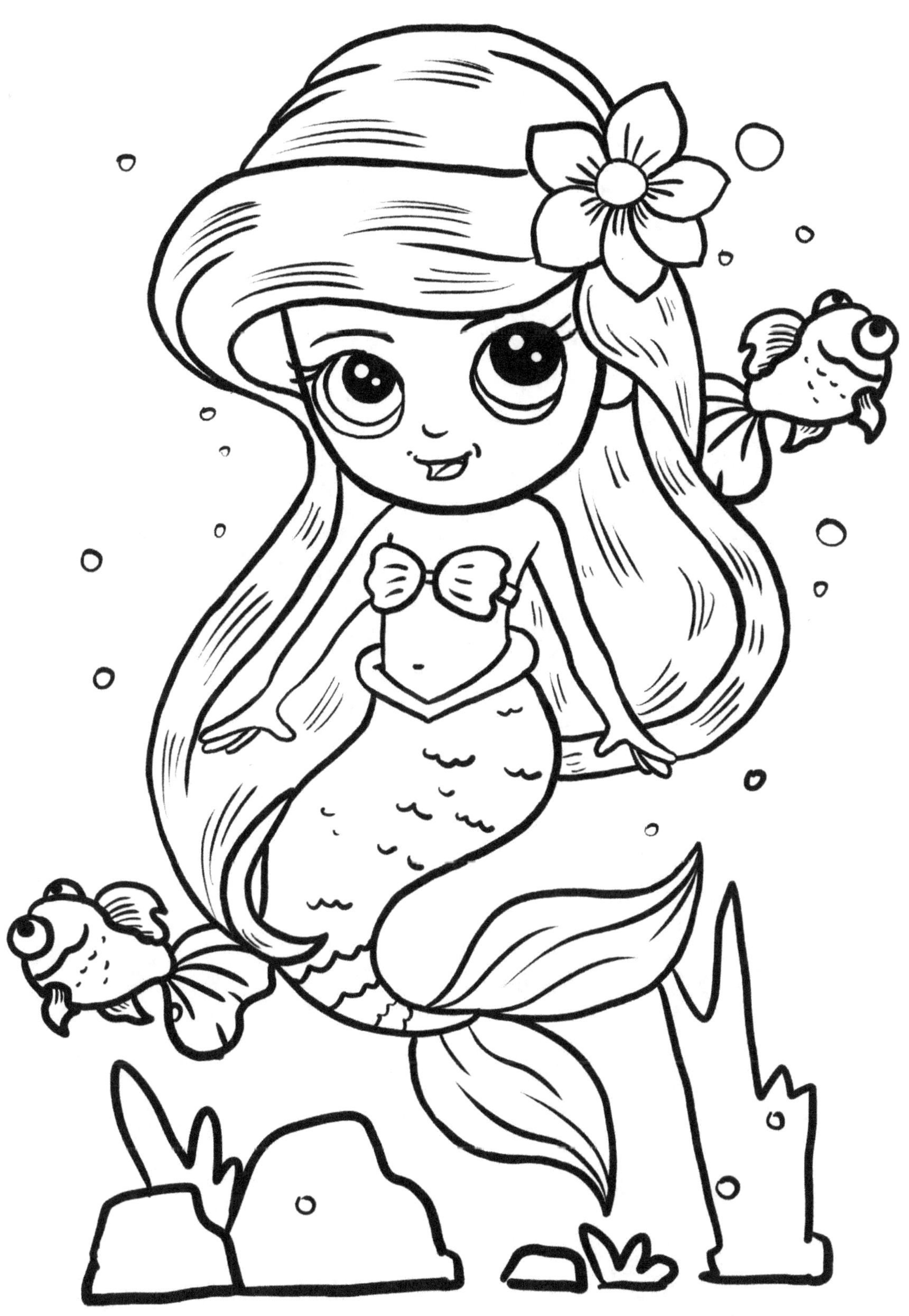

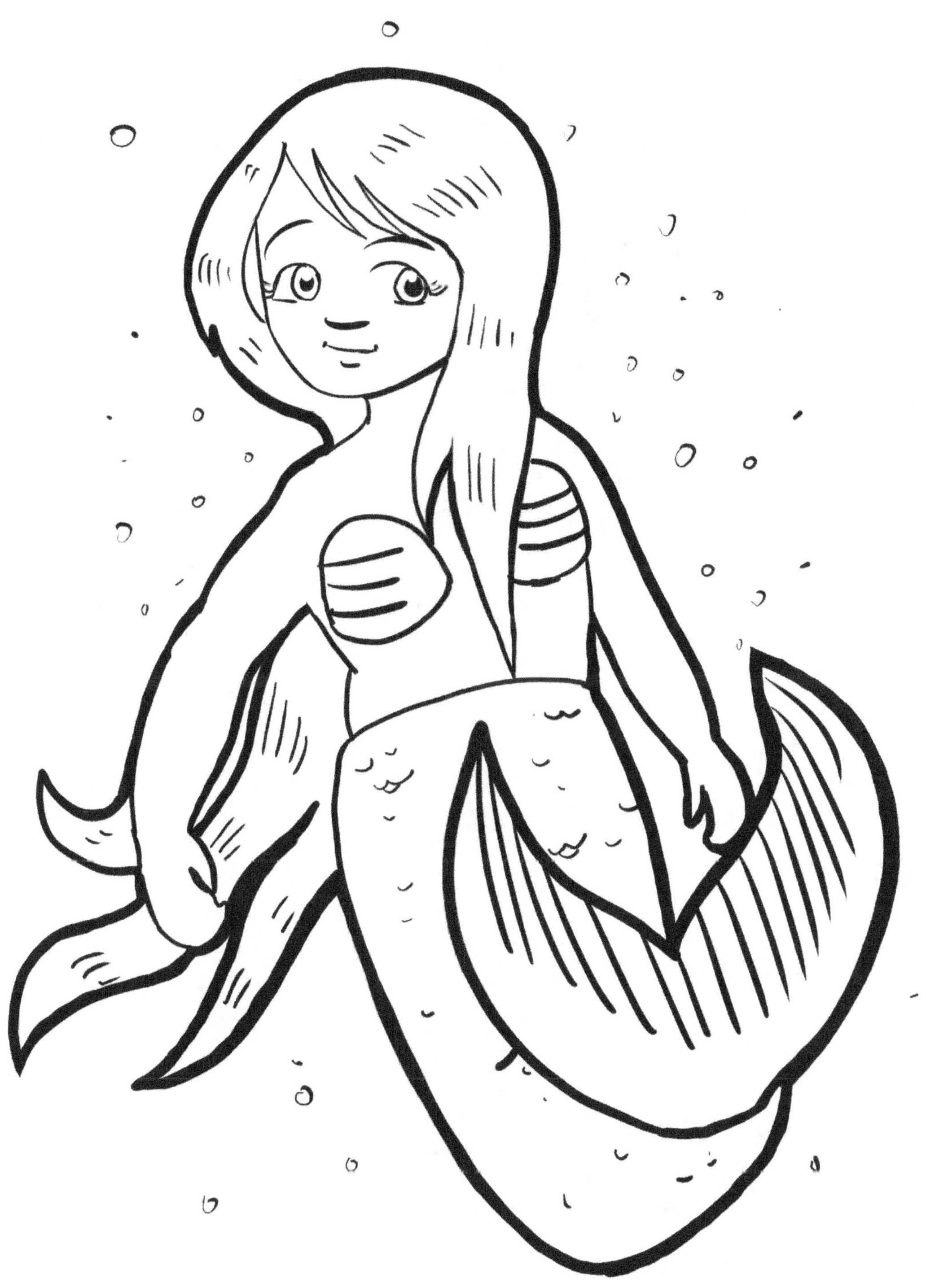

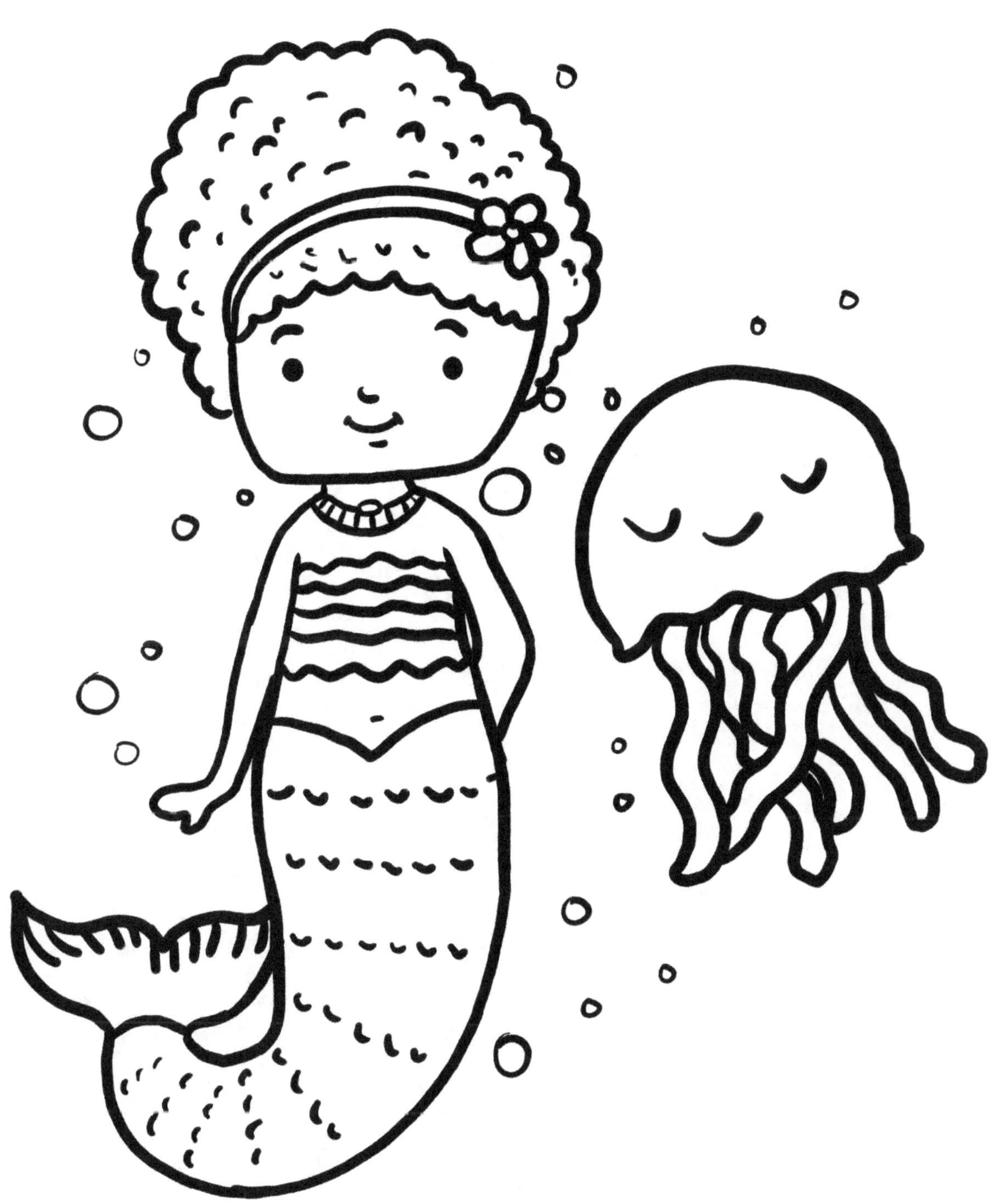

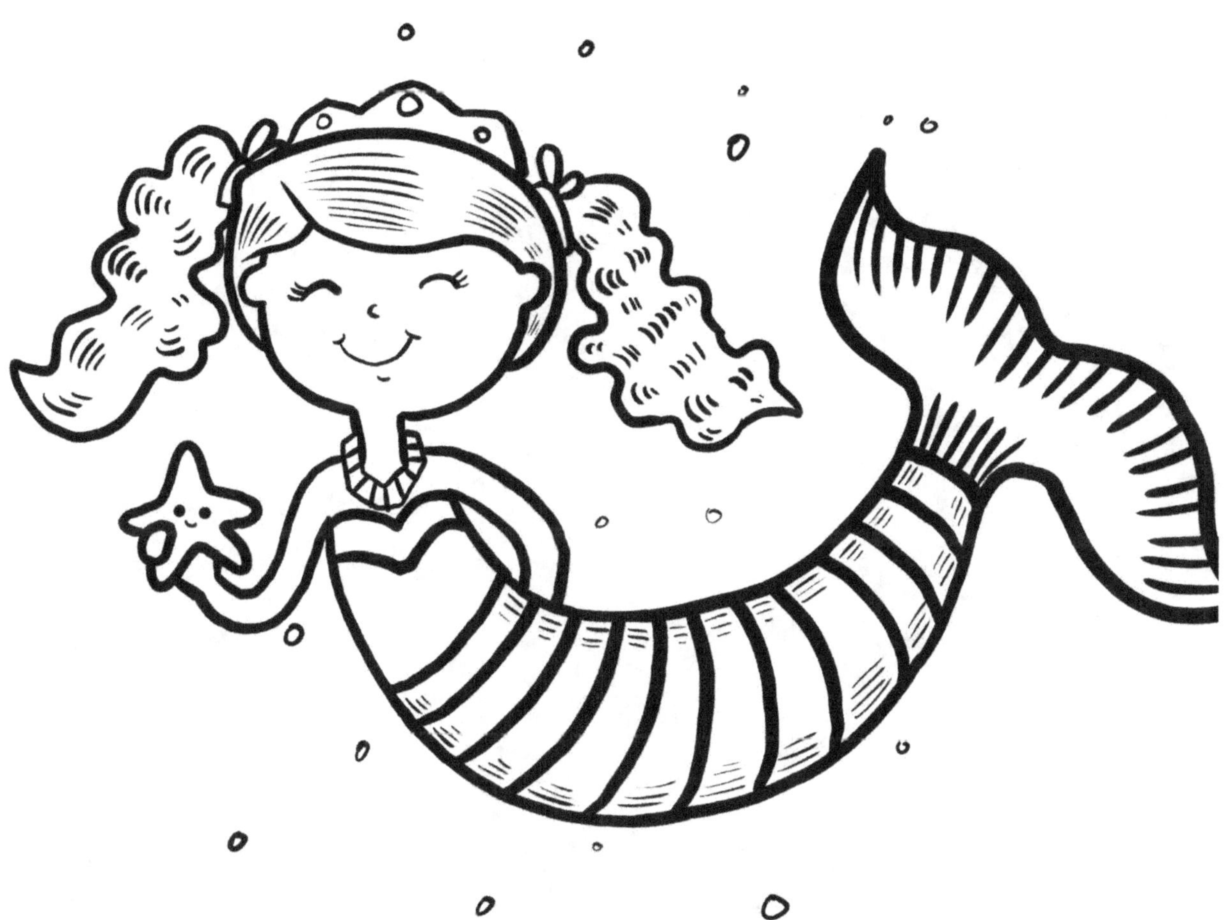

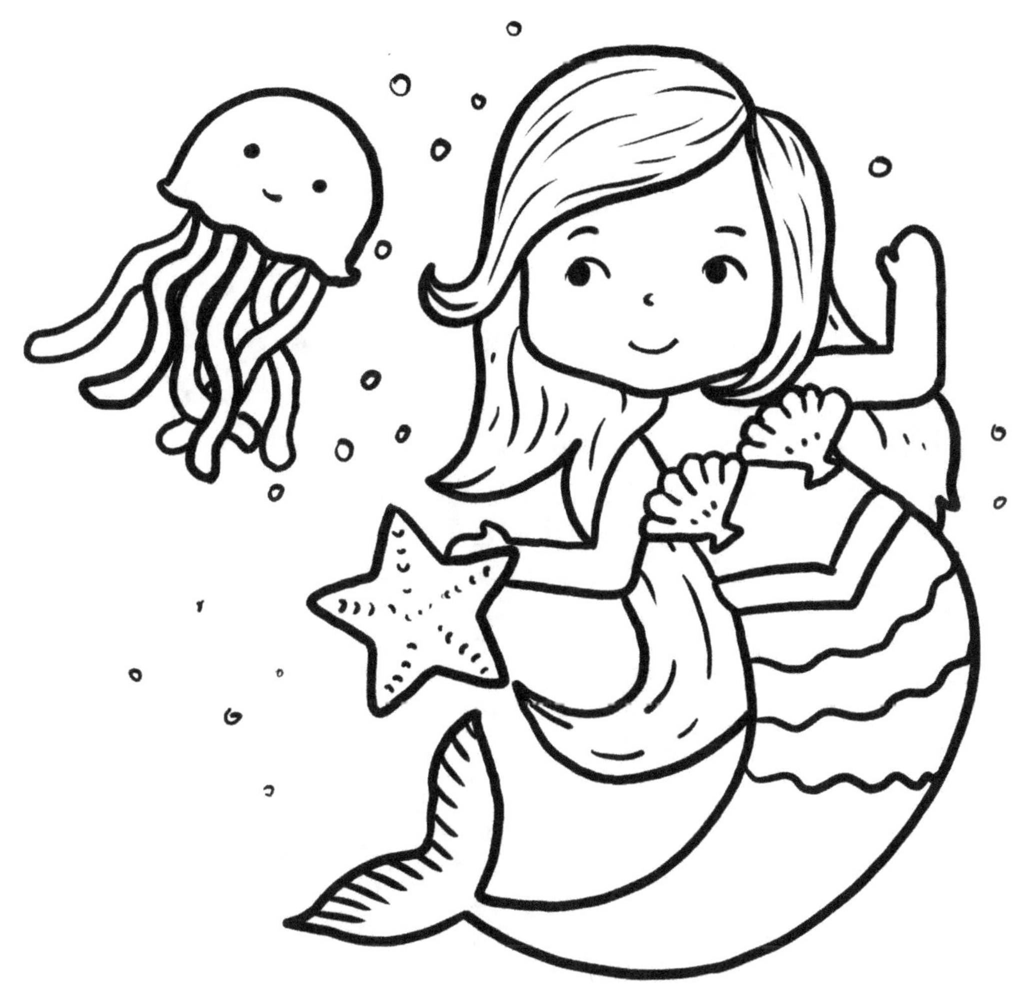

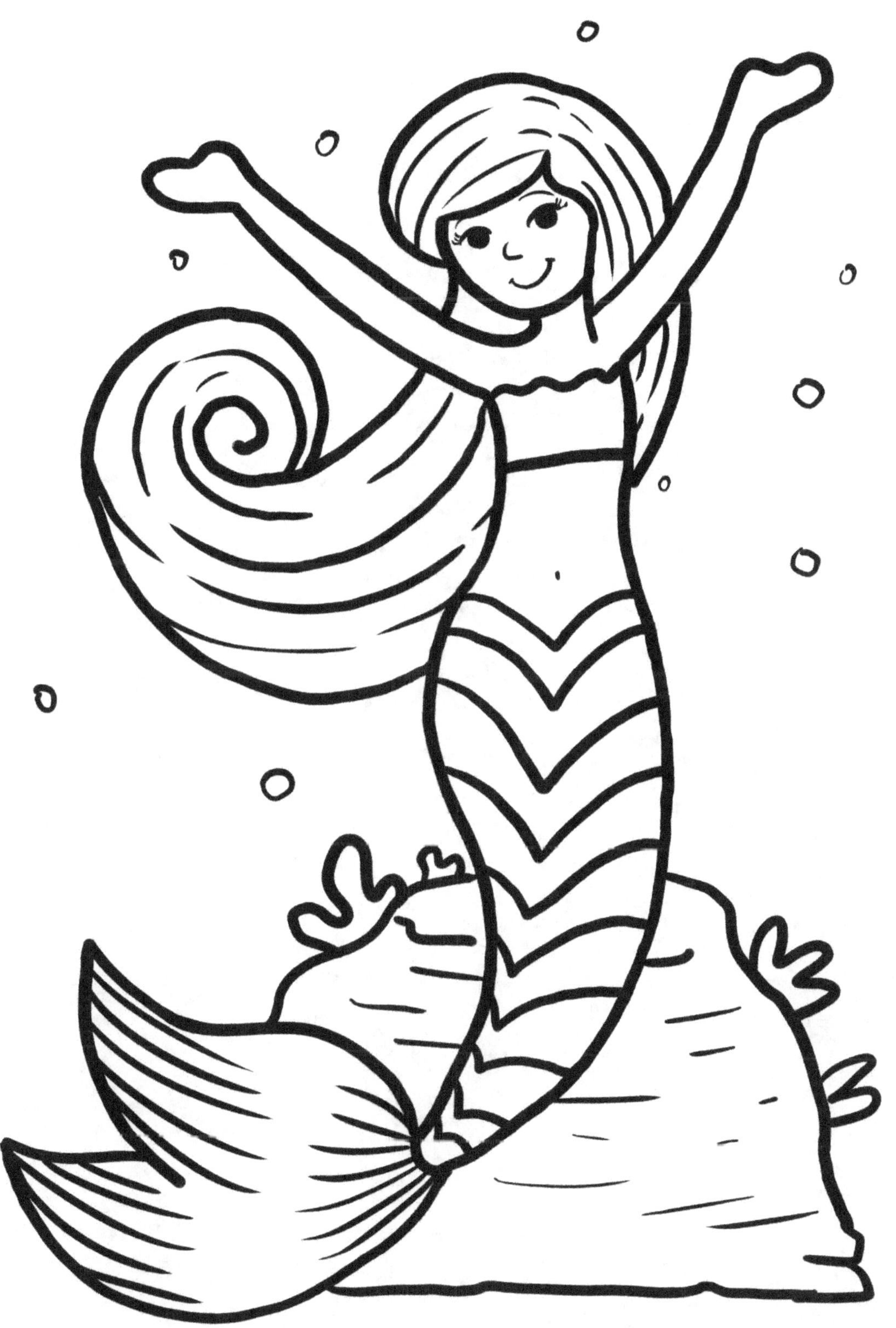

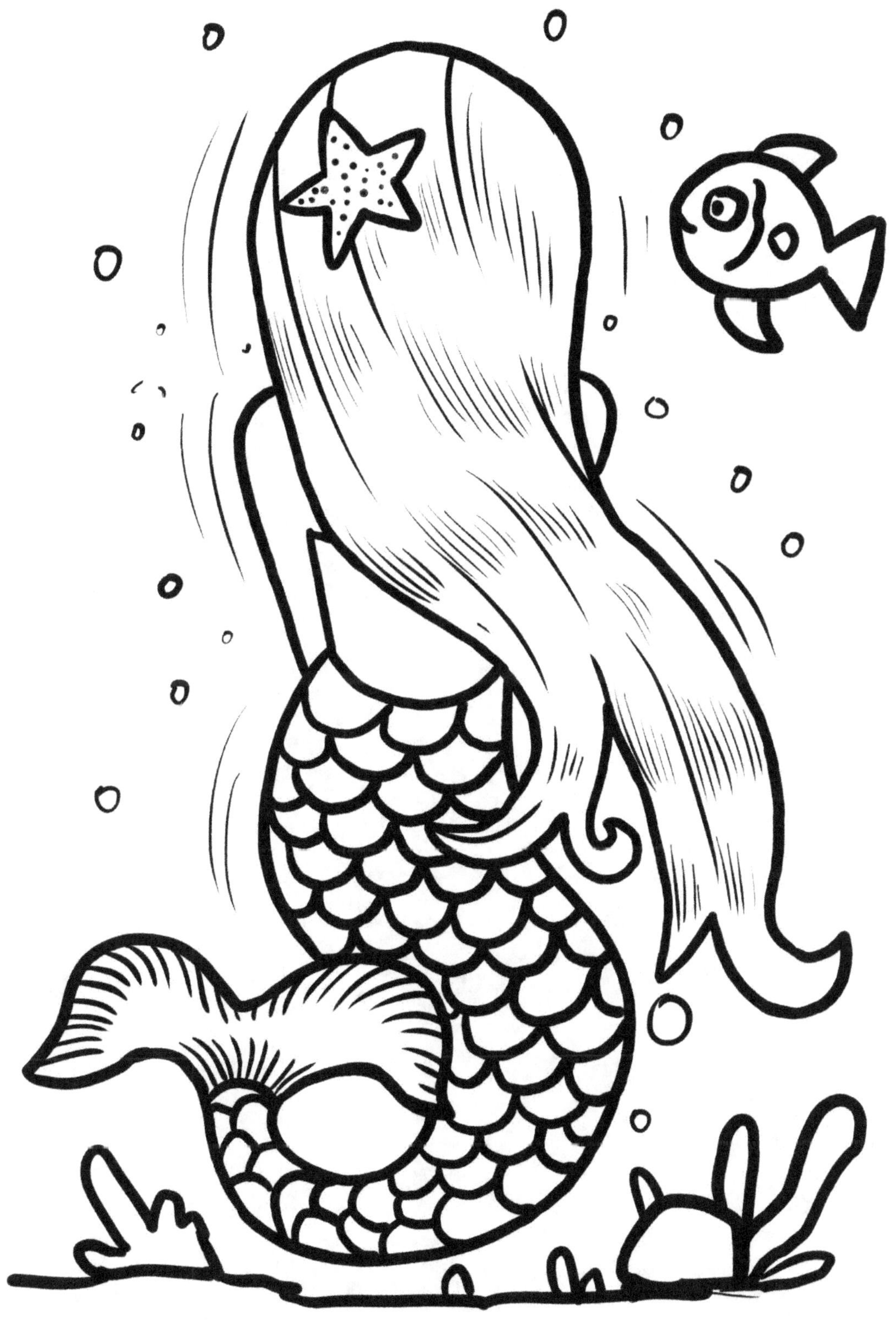

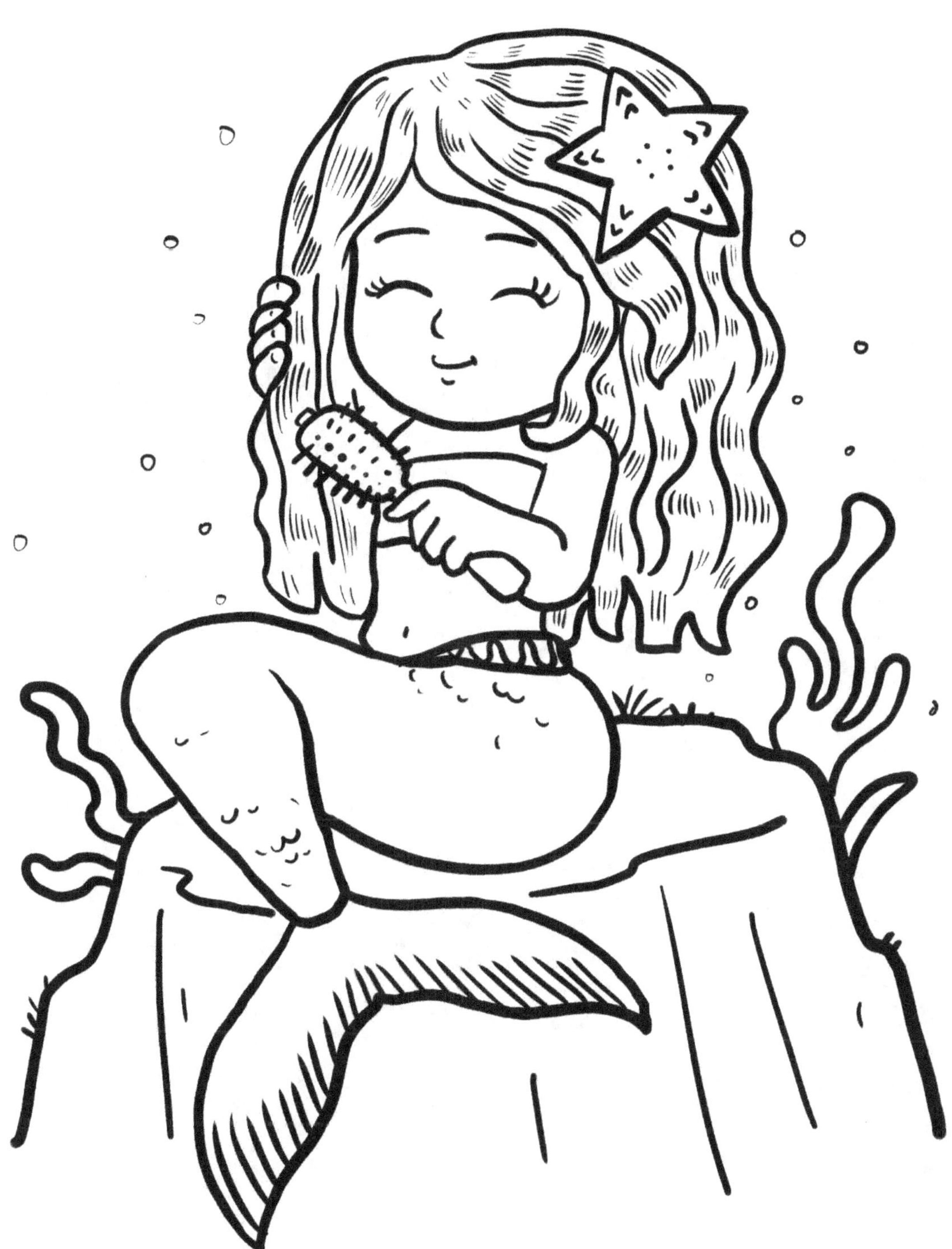

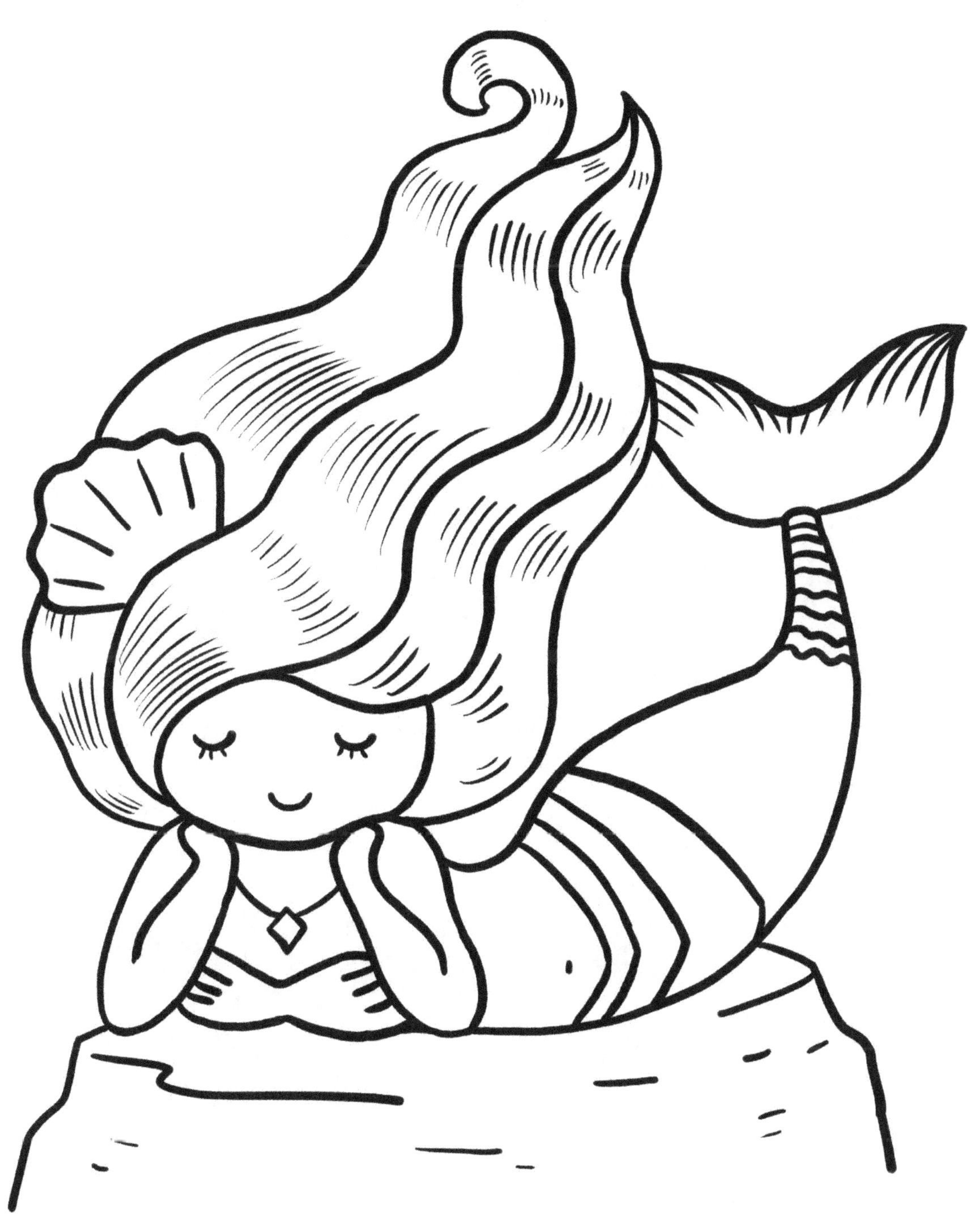

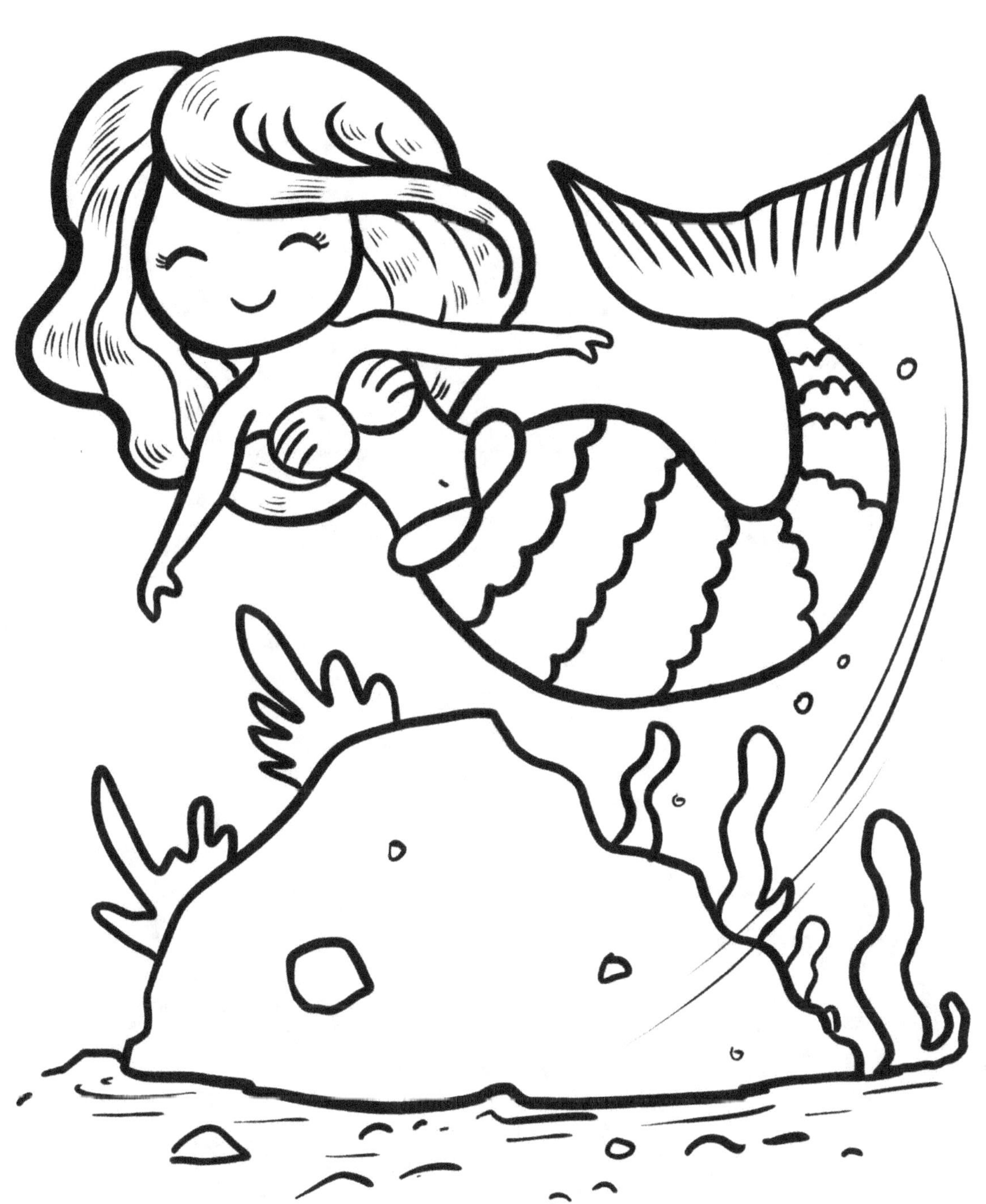

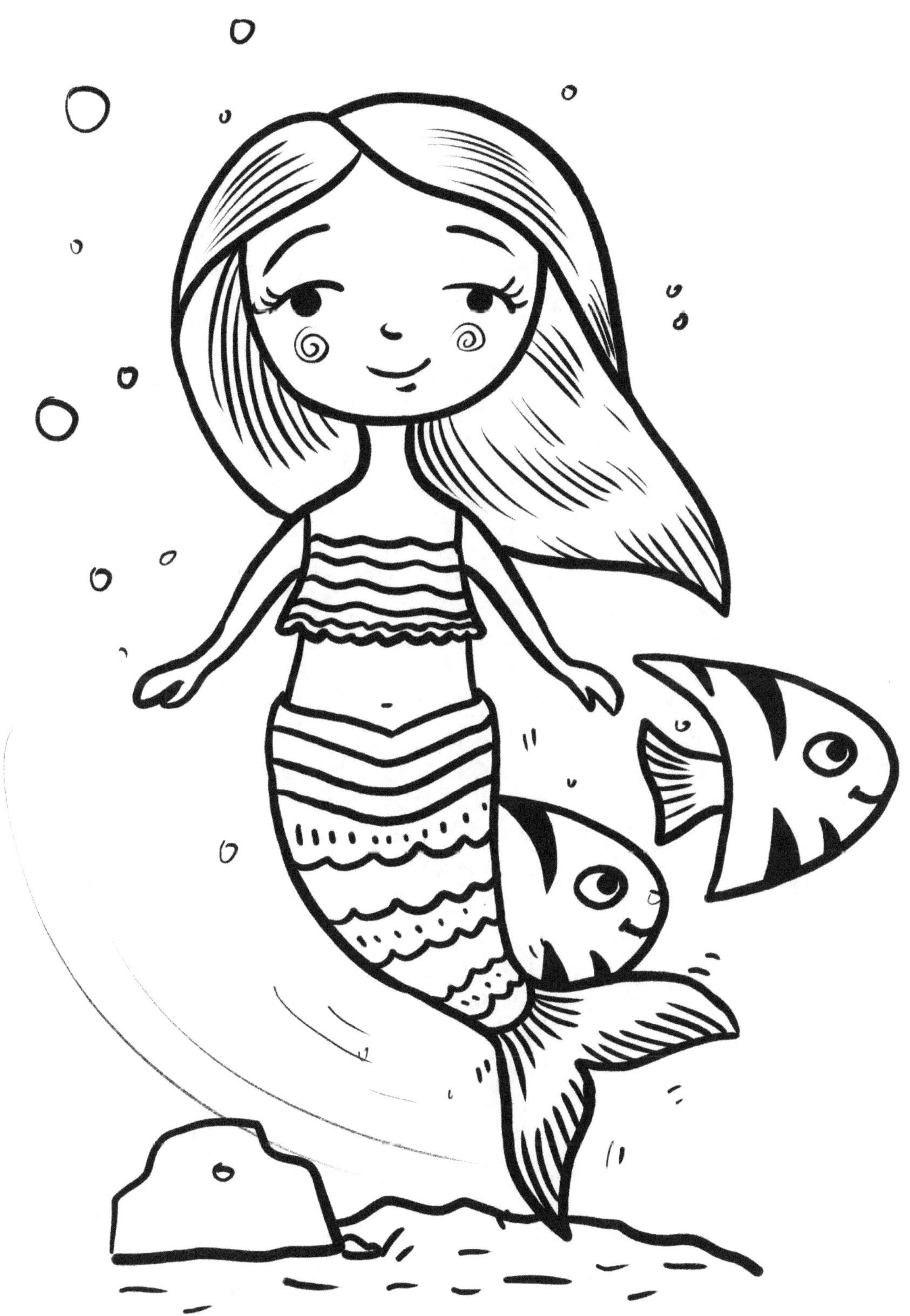

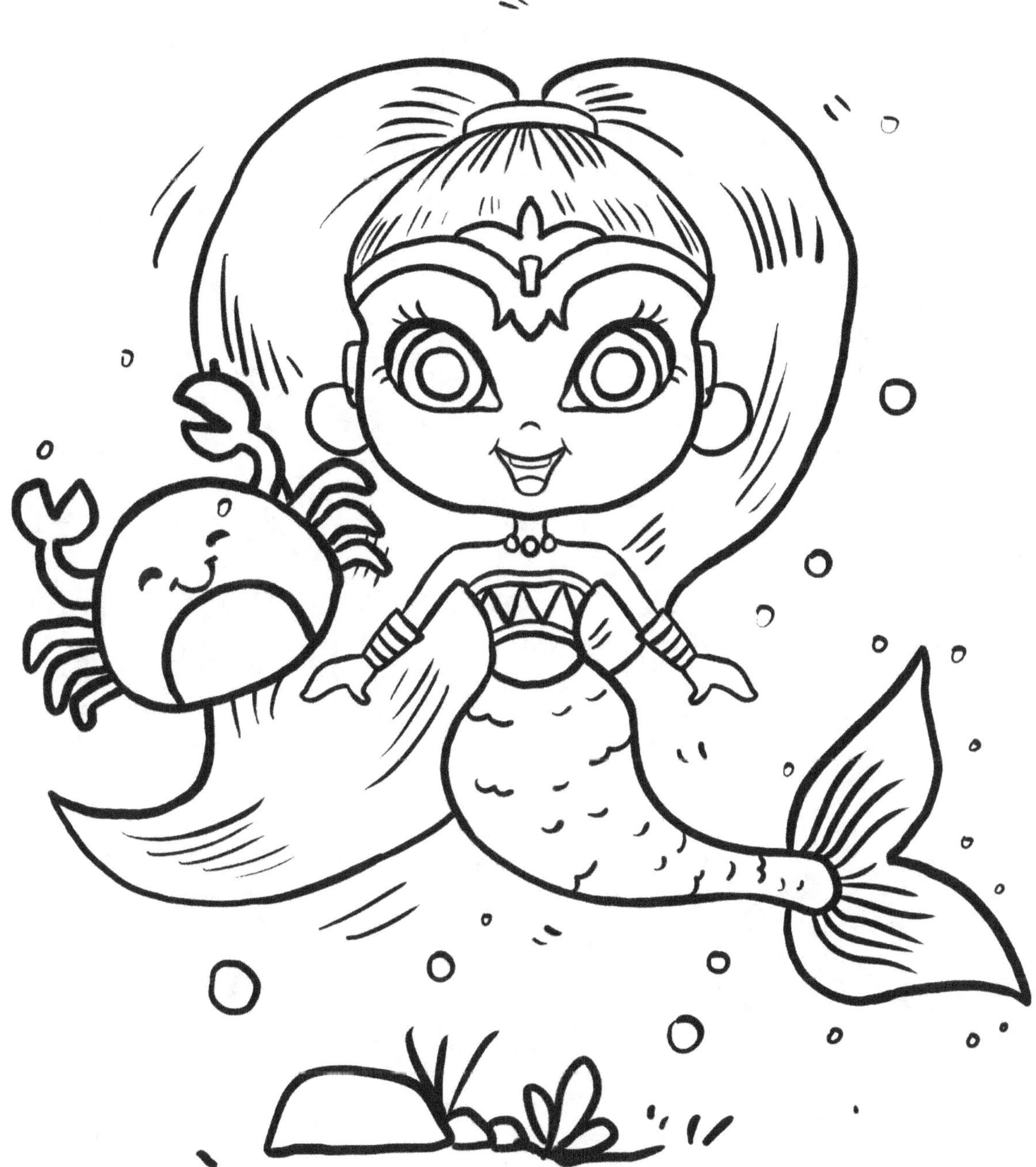

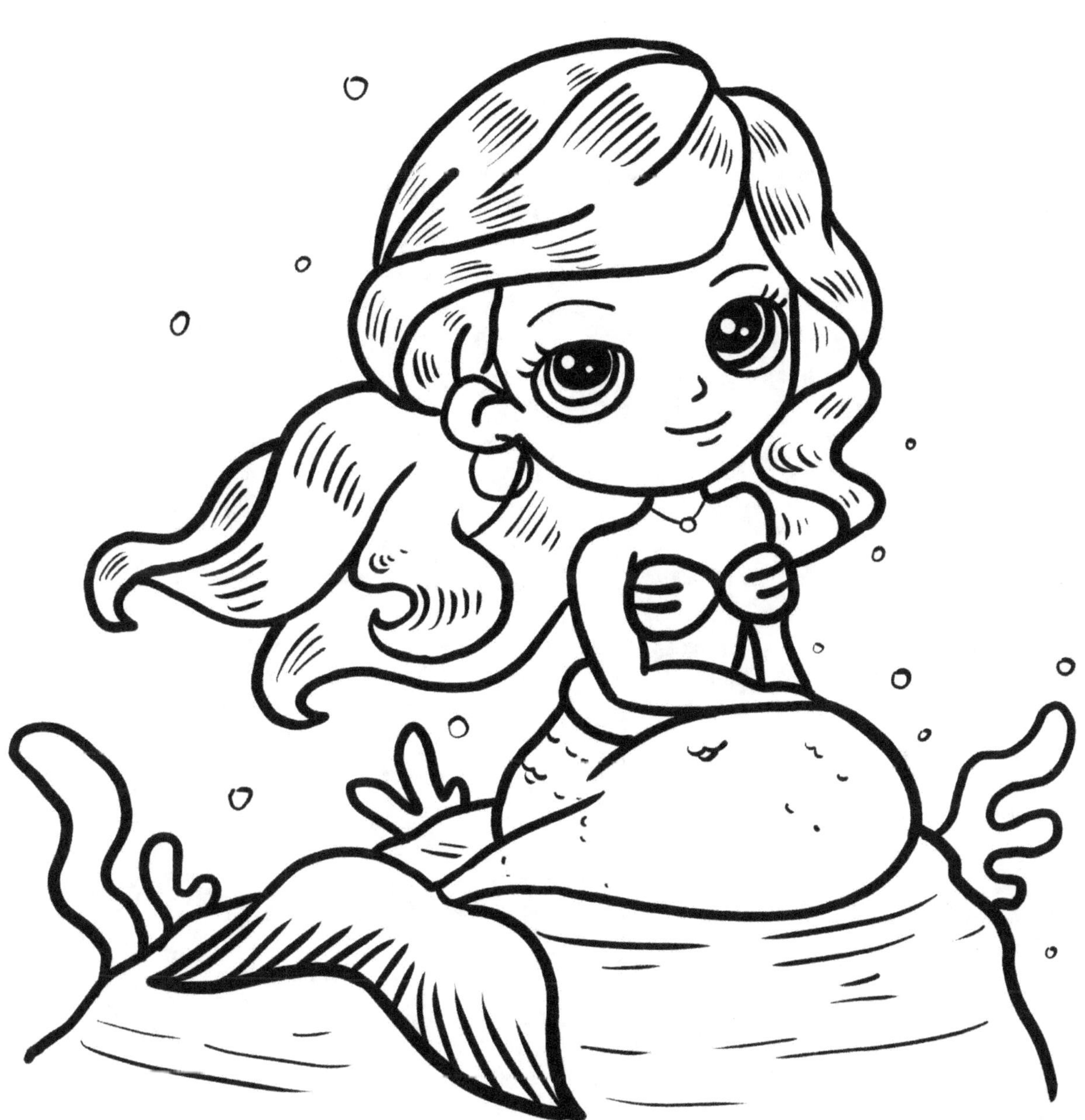

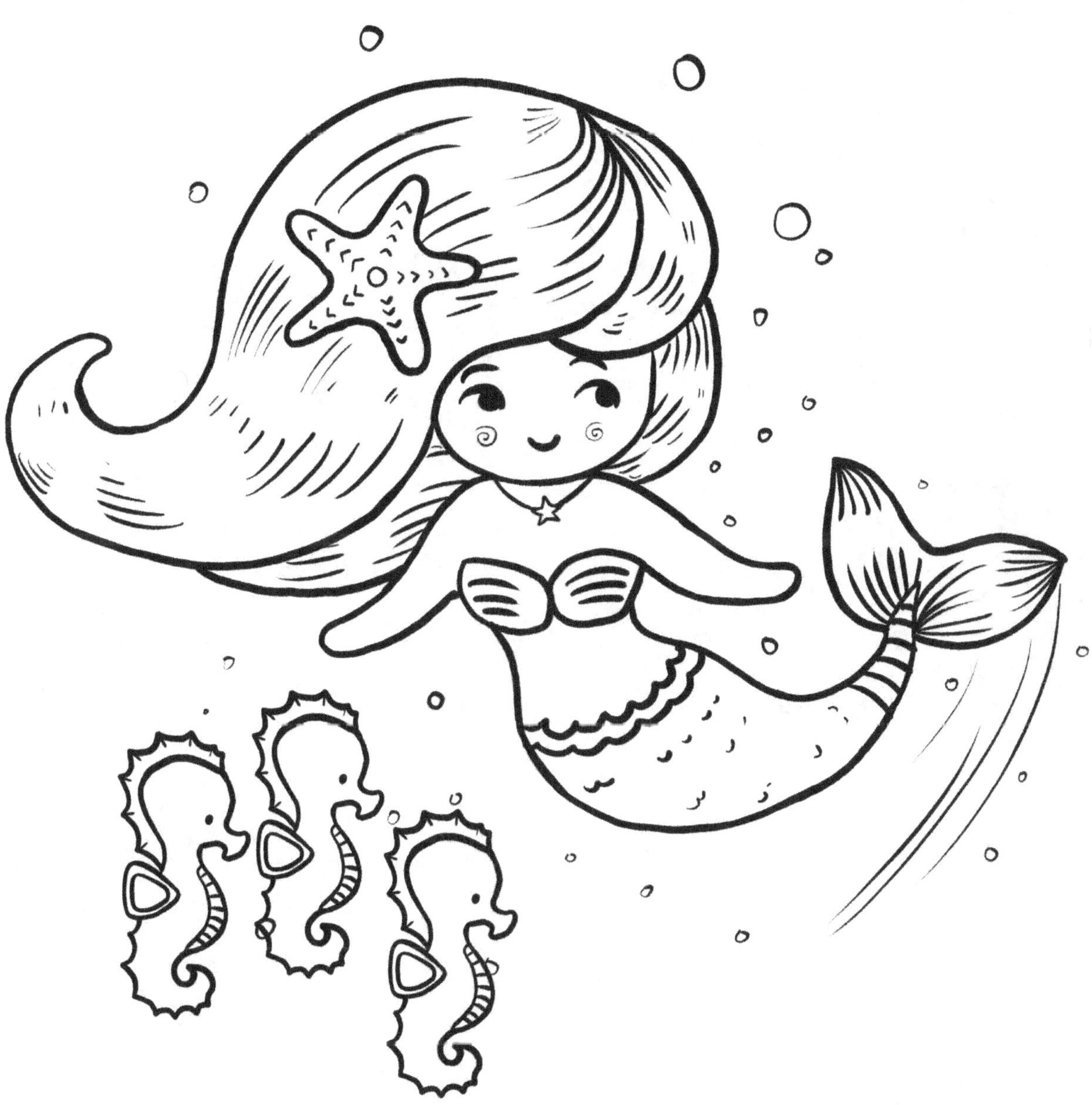

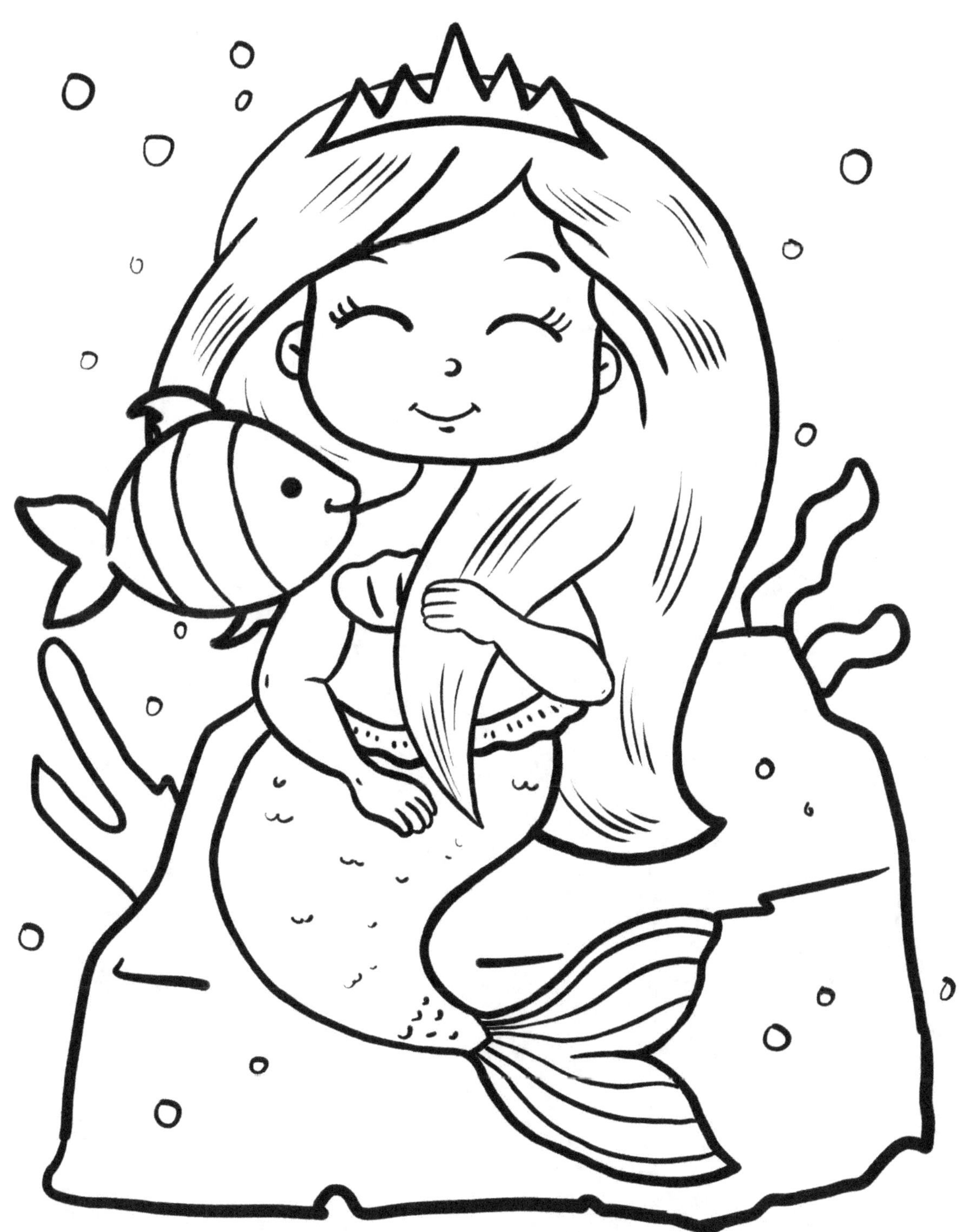

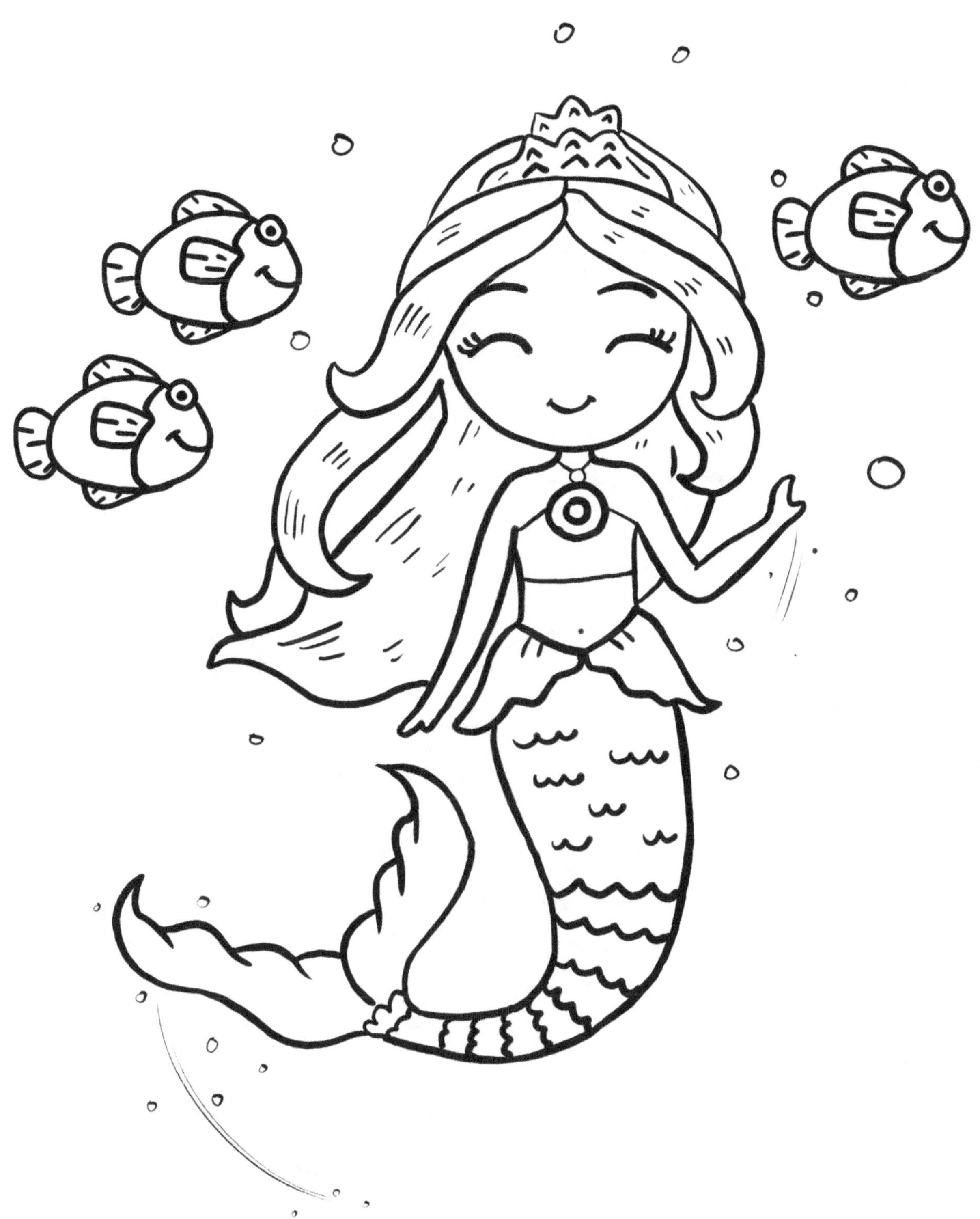

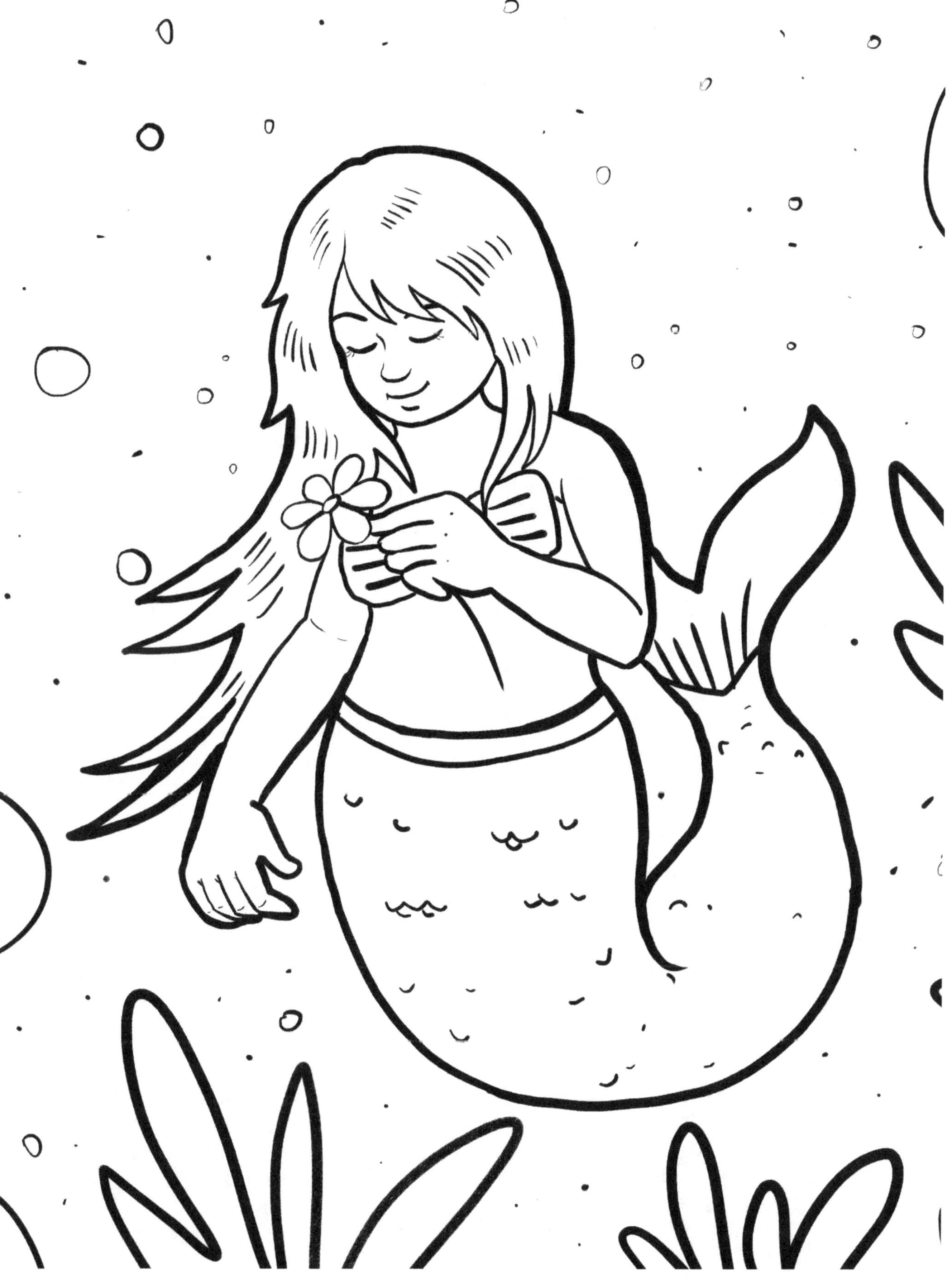

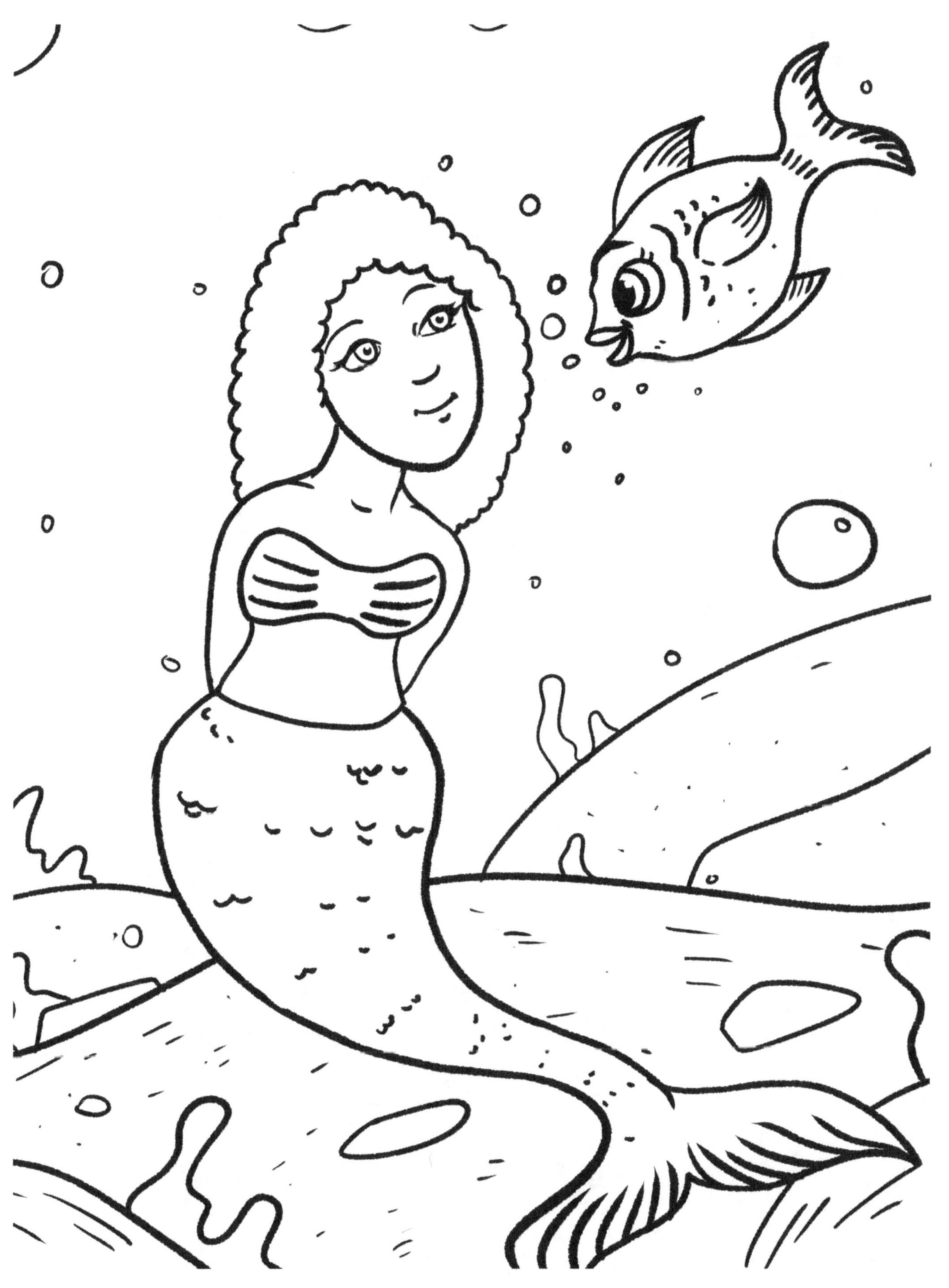

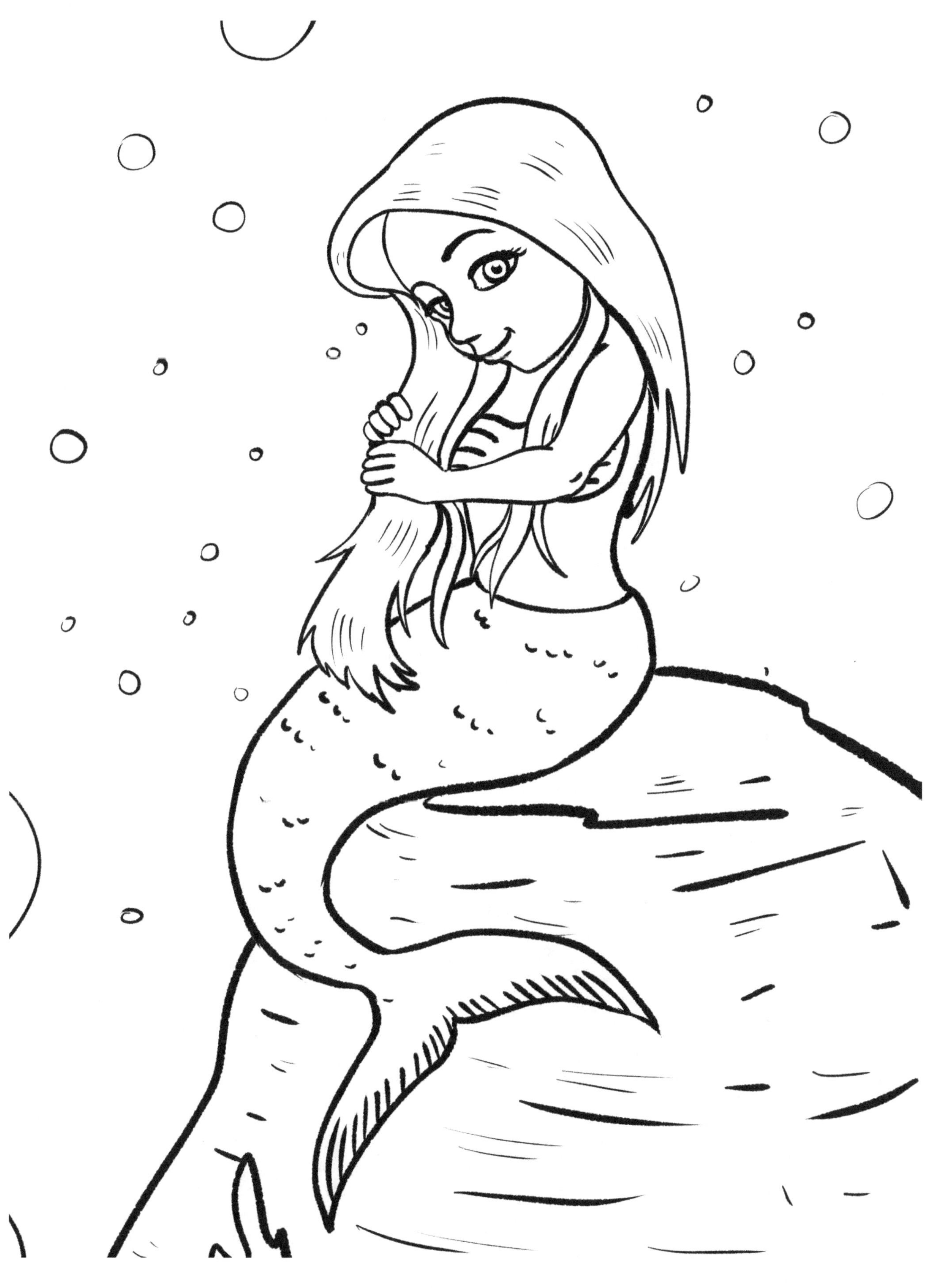

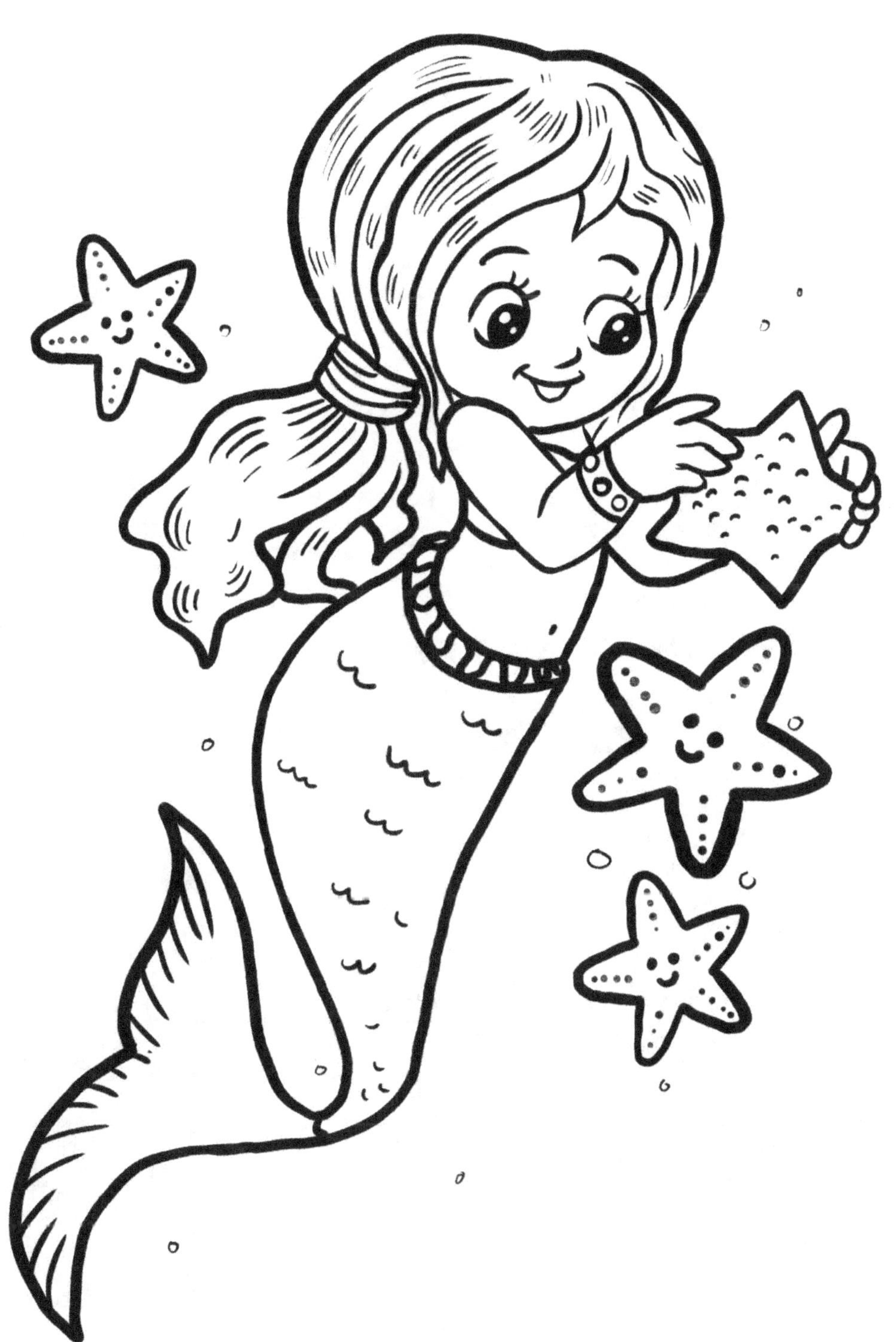

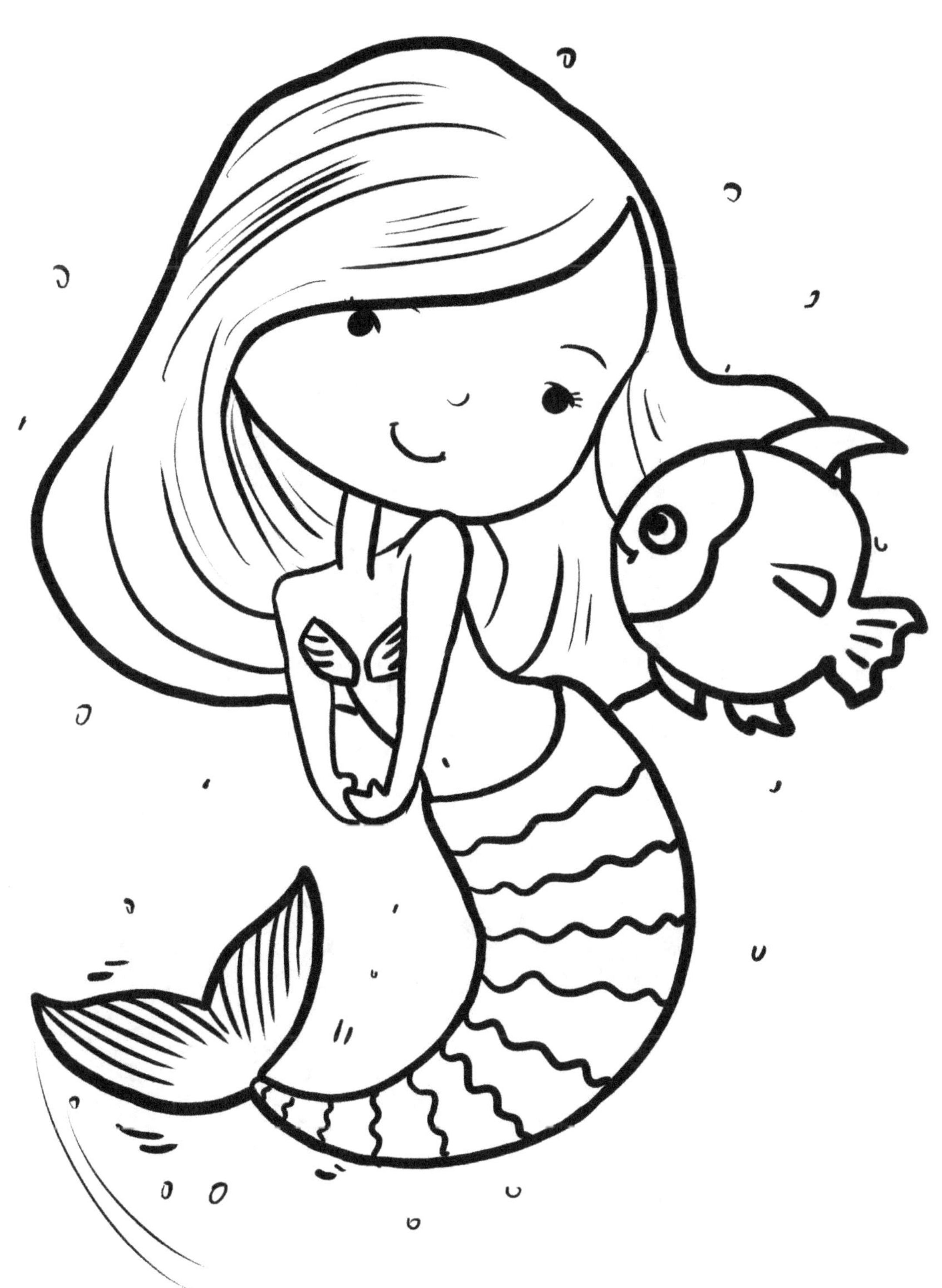

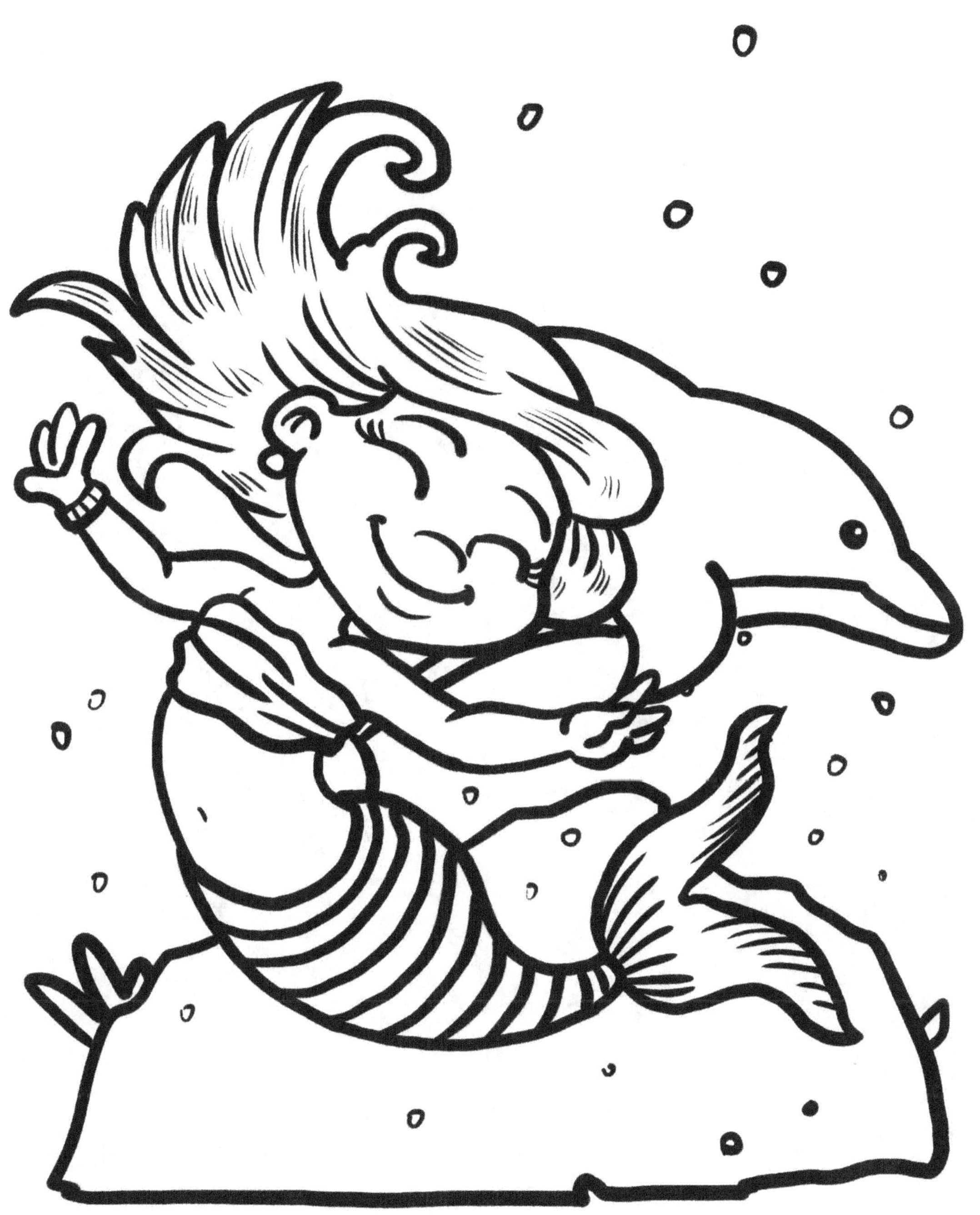

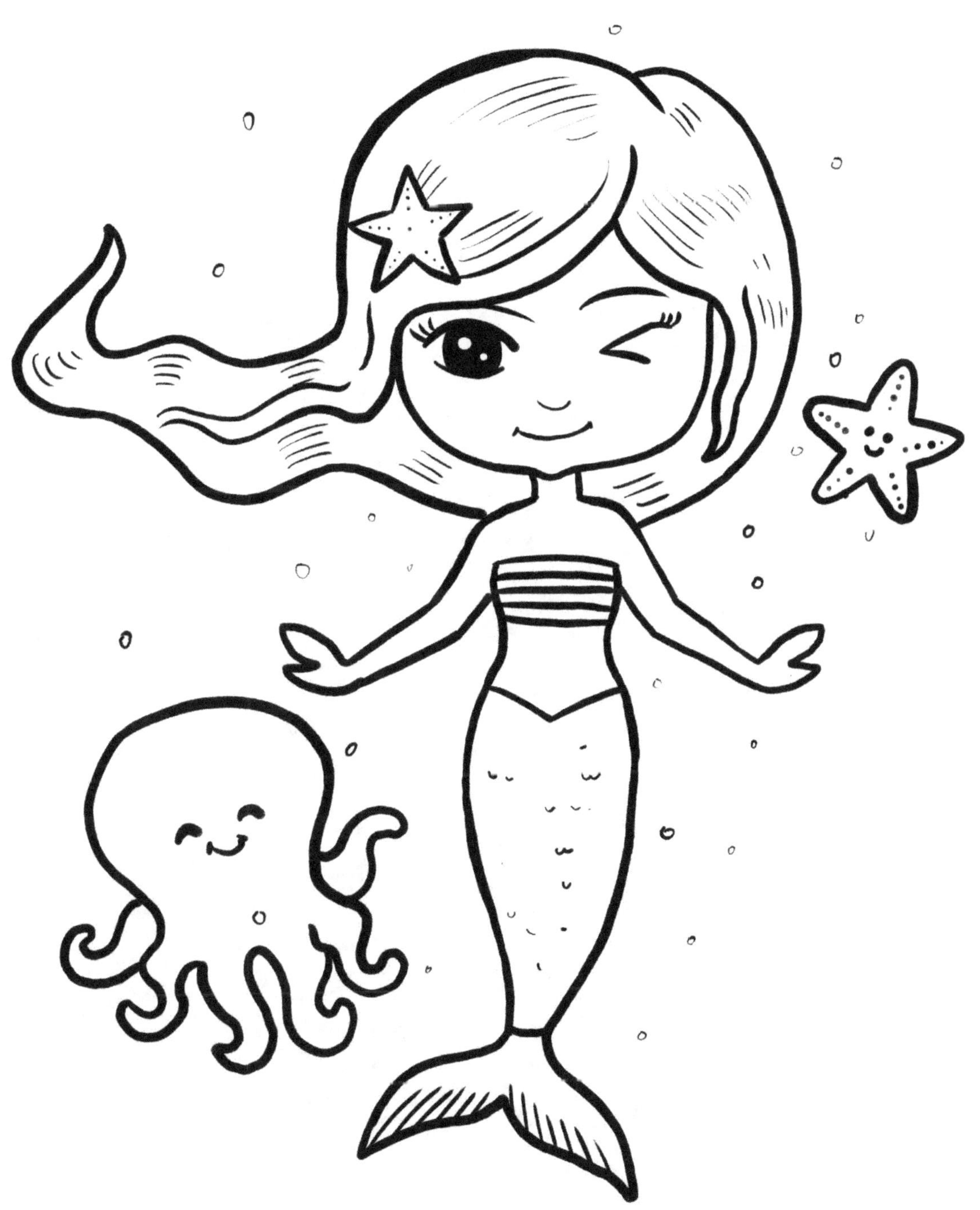